BLAIRS
P9-DBP-308

DATE DUE

DEC 16			
JAN 2 5 1974			
APR 2 5 1974			
FEB 7 1975			
APR 2 9 1975			
MAY 1 4 1975			
DEC 3			
DEC 17			
JAN 8			
JAN 29			
FEB 13			
MAR 2			
MAR 18			

GAYLORD PRINTED IN U.S.A.

The United States Department of

THE TREASURY

BLAIRSVILLE SENIOR HIGH SCHOOL
BLAIRSVILLE, PENNA.

Books by JOHN UPTON TERRELL

JEAN BLUE

ADAM CARGO

PLUME ROUGE

THE KEY TO WASHINGTON

THE LITTLE DARK MAN

SUNDAY IS THE DAY YOU REST

JOURNEY INTO DARKNESS

FURS BY ASTOR

THE UNITED STATES DEPARTMENT OF THE INTERIOR:
A Story of Rangeland, Wildlife, and Dams

THE UNITED STATES DEPARTMENT OF THE TREASURY:
A Story of Dollars, Customs, and Secret Agents

In Preparation

THE UNITED STATES DEPARTMENT OF STATE

The United States Department of
THE TREASURY

A Story of Dollars, Customs, and Secret Agents

BY

JOHN UPTON TERRELL

BLAIRSVILLE SENIOR HIGH SCHOOL
BLAIRSVILLE, PENNA.

DUELL, SLOAN AND PEARCE
New York

6927

COPYRIGHT © 1963 BY JOHN UPTON TERRELL

All rights reserved. No part of this book in excess of five hundred words may be reproduced in any form without permission in writing from the publisher.

First Edition

Affiliate of
MEREDITH PRESS
Des Moines & New York

Library of Congress Catalogue Card Number: 63-16833

MANUFACTURED IN THE UNITED STATES OF AMERICA FOR MEREDITH PRESS

VAN REES PRESS • NEW YORK

CONTENTS

The United States Department of
THE TREASURY

I

GUARDIAN OF THE PUBLIC WEALTH

THE Treasury Department affects the life of every person in the United States.

Its activities are anything but dull, for it is not simply an enormous office in which humdrum bookkeeping and routine accounting are carried on. To the contrary, its duties are rife with intrigue, mystery, and drama.

Each of its many functions is founded on money, which certainly is important to everyone, but it is not only the collecting and spending of money that occupies the time of Treasury employees.

Eight police forces, some of them world renowned, are under the supervision of the Treasury Department: the Secret Service, the Bureau of Narcotics, Customs inspectors, Intelligence agents, Alcohol Revenue agents, Internal Security Division, White House Police, and Treasury Guards. The Treasury has its own navy—the famous United States Coast Guard.

In these arenas of action there is never a dull moment. They are marked continually by violence, cruelty, dishonesty, bloodshed, and often with death.

The Treasury is older than the United States of America.

Its history reaches back into the smoke and fury of the Revolutionary War.

When the American Colonies began their struggle for independence from England, they had no organized central government. They were bound together by nothing stronger than the silken strand of a great principle—freedom and justice for every man.

A Continental Congress was called together in Philadelphia. Its chief task and most difficult problem was to find money to meet the terrible cost of the war. The Congress had no power to tax people, for the thirteen colonial governments, jealous of their own rights, had refused to surrender that power. Nor could the Continental Congress expect to borrow money from foreign countries, for it had no credit standing and it did not represent an actual nation which might be held responsible for its debts.

Faced with this vital problem, the members of the Continental Congress took the only road they saw open to them. They voted to print paper money in the form of "promises to pay." That is, each note was actually an I O U. It was a dangerous thing to do, for there was no way to guarantee the people who gave money for the I O U's that they would be repaid in full. All the Congress could do was pledge the faith and courage of the ragged patriots who were then defying the superior British troops on the field of battle.

Bad conditions already had made paper money issued by some of the colonies virtually worthless, and businessmen and farmers had suffered bitter losses, but the people generally believed in the justice of the revolutionary cause, they were convinced that victory would be theirs, and they approved of the action the Congress had voted to take.

Only a few days after the Battle of Bunker Hill, on July 23, 1775, Richard Bache, Stephen Pascall, and Michael Hillegas were appointed to superintend the printing of two million dollars, and the Congress employed twenty-eight trustworthy citizens of Philadelphia to sign and number the notes.

This was the beginning of the Treasury.

A few days later, in that same month of July, the Congress took another important step in the difficult task of paying the heavy costs of the Revolution. It appointed two joint treasurers of the United Colonies. They were Michael Hillegas and George Clymer, and it was their responsibility to manage the government's finances.

These two men were the first treasurers of the great republic which was then in the process of being born.

For the first time, the Colonies had obligated themselves together in a public debt. In order that each colony would pay its just share, and no more or no less, the Congress ordered that a population census be taken.

In time more millions of dollars were printed, and to be sure that it was being spent wisely and not wasted, the Congress named a committee to superintend the Treasury, examine all accounts, and submit regular reports. On the committee were the distinguished Americans James Duane, Elbridge Gerry, Richard Smith, Thomas Nelson, and Thomas Willing.

Still not satisfied that it had done all in its power to safeguard the public finances, the Congress resolved that a Treasury Office of Accounts be set up to operate under the direction of the Treasury Committee. All bills against the United Colonies were to be presented to this office, and an auditor general and a staff of competent clerks were to keep strict account of every penny taken in and paid out.

This was the beginning of the orderly and accurate accounting system that is still carried on in the great gray Treasury Building in Washington. In all the years since the Revolutionary War there has never been a day when the Treasury did not know to the penny how much money the nation possessed, never a day when it was not known exactly how much had been paid out, never a day when the Treasury books did not show precisely how much the Government owed and how much money people owed it.

During the remainder of the Revolution, and in the years immediately after it, the Treasury was under the direction of various committees and executives. It was not until September, 1789—thirteen years after the signing of the Declaration of Independence and six years after the United States had been recognized as a nation by the Treaty of Paris—that the Department of the Treasury we know today was established by Congress.

President Washington named his former aide-de-camp, Alexander Hamilton, as the first Secretary of the Treasury. It was a wise choice. Hamilton was a brilliant, able, and devoted public servant. He was a believer in a strong central government. Much of his time was allotted to organizing and expanding the work of the Customs collectors and to establishing a simplified and centralized government purchasing system. He was the founder of the Coast Guard. He held a vision of a future America as a wealthy industrial nation. No better illustration of Hamilton's rare perspicacity and commercial genius exists than the accuracy of that vision.

Hamilton met a tragic death. He was killed in 1804 in a duel with Aaron Burr, whom he had vigorously opposed when Burr sought election to the presidency and to the governorship of New York. He left an enduring legacy to the United States. A bronze statue of him, sculptured by James Earle Fraser, stands at the foot of the south steps of the Treasury Building in Washington, and on it is the inscription:

Soldier Orator Statesman
Champion of Constitutional Union
Representative Government and
National Integrity .

Today the Secretary of the Treasury is the chief financial officer of the Government, just as he was in Hamilton's time. More than fifty Secretaries have held office since 1789. Not all of them were men of great distinction and ability, but each of them left his mark, be it small or large, in the annals of the great department that has influenced so decisively the growth and prosperity of America and played such a vital part in national affairs.

The story of the Treasury, however, is not only history. It is a story of the present moment, and because what the Treasury does today will have a great bearing on the future of the United States, it is the story of tomorrow.

II

CUSTOMS AND SMUGGLERS

Not long ago an airline pilot landed a big transport at an eastern airport after a flight from Europe and walked calmly down the landing steps at the head of a long line of passengers. Two agents of the Bureau of Customs quickly stepped forward and quietly arrested him.

In their airport office the Customs men took $233,000 worth of diamonds from the pilot's pockets.

The pilot, who had no previous criminal record, was one of the thousands of people who try each year to outwit the agents of the Bureau of Customs and smuggle valuable goods into the United States. Most of them are caught and are sent to jail or pay heavy fines. Only a comparatively small number of them can be classed as members of the underworld. The majority are normally law-abiding citizens who cannot resist the temptation to sneak merchandise into the country and escape the payment of an import tax.

The odds of success are heavily against both the amateur and the professional smuggler. What they seem to forget, or perhaps choose to ignore, is the fact that the Customs men are usually informed when an attempt to bring goods into the country illegally is to be made. This was true in the case of the airline pilot, and it has been true in countless other attempts that have failed.

Last year more than 150,000,000 civilian travelers passed through Customs at the many ports of the United States. They brought with them more than $15,000,000,000 worth of foreign merchandise of every conceivable kind that required handling by Customs men. Hundreds of ships arrived from foreign ports with cargoes that had to be checked. At American airports more than 167,000 airplanes engaged in international travel landed with goods and passengers from abroad. In addition to this enormous traffic, more than 43,000,000 automobiles crossed our borders from Canada and Mexico.

It was a staggering flood of imports and people. Searching every person and every package would have been impossible. The Bureau of Customs would have needed at least 50,000 inspectors to have performed an adequate job. Yet, the Bureau has only 8,500 employees in all its branches. Some 270 work in the Washington headquarters. The rest are distributed in seaports, border and interior ports, and international airports, and many of these men and women perform office and other administrative duties. There are only 3,200 supervising Customs agents, inspectors, and patrol officers directly engaged in inspecting baggage, cargoes, and travelers in the whole of the United States!

The success of the Bureau of Customs in disrupting the flow of illicit traffic is truly remarkable. It stems chiefly from three sources: long and thorough training of inspectors, years of experience, and informants.

New Customs agents are sent to a special training school. There they are given courses in modern investigative techniques, such as how to search vessels, planes, and cars for contraband, how to question travelers and examine luggage, and how to expose the tricks with which people constantly try to fool them, most of which are as old as the Customs Bureau itself.

The Bureau estimates that it takes five years to train a man or woman to be an efficient Customs examiner. In that time most inspectors become expert in sniffing out attempts at smuggling. They are thoroughly familiar with all the schemes used by small and large smugglers, and the old hands have an uncanny knack for spotting such things as concealed compartments in luggage, hollowed-out heels of shoes, bellybands or false belts worn under clothing, and double pockets.

Inspectors have spotted gems hidden in crutches, golf clubs, billiard cues, shaving brush handles, fountain pens, toothpaste, bottles of medicine, and even in chewing gum, glass eyes, and false teeth.

Informants in foreign countries are invaluable to the Bureau of Customs. They not only tip off the agents about the activities of professional criminals, but about the respectable traveler who might attempt to smuggle in a diamond ring, a camera, a Swiss watch, or even goods for suits and dresses on which a duty must be paid.

As a reward for their services, informers receive 25 per cent of the value of any goods seized. This reward makes it well worth their while to co-operate with the Customs men, and some of them have become well-to-do through such undercover work.

As an example, suppose an American woman traveler in France buys an emerald necklace. The clerk in the shop where the purchase was made quietly goes to the nearest American Embassy or Consulate and registers the woman's name and the amount paid for the jewels. If the woman does not tell about her purchase and pay duty on it when she arrives in the United States, she is arrested. If the necklace is valued at $4,000, the informant receives a reward of $1,000. Thousands of clerks and shopowners in foreign countries report sales made to Americans in the hope of getting such rewards. This makes it very difficult for the amateur smuggler to be successful.

The Customs inspectors have nine laboratories to assist them in determining the value of goods brought into the country either by legal or illegal means. Men and women who are expert judges of the quality of virtually every type of merchandise are employed by the Treasury, and there are more than 5,000 categories into which dutiable imports fall—a staggering number for an inspector to keep in mind.

Let us study briefly two cases, taken from official reports, which show how Customs inspectors work.

In one of the cases, the Customs Office in New York City received information from the Bureau's London office that the chief steward on the S.S. *Assyria*, which was then en route to the United States, would attempt to smuggle a large quantity of diamonds and deliver them to confederates in a New York hotel. The ship arrived, and when the steward went ashore he was followed by Customs agents. He made no attempt to pass on the diamonds, and in time he was taken into custody and questioned. He denied that he was engaged in smuggling, but an alert agent spotted information in the steward's papers which indicated he was connected with several known law violators. The agents searched the steward's cabin and the quarters in which he performed his duties on the ship, but no diamonds were found.

After the vessel had sailed from New York on a voyage along the American coast, the New York agents were informed that the diamonds were still on board. The ship returned to New York, and once more the agents shadowed the chief steward, but he made no attempt to land the diamonds or to get in touch with his confederates.

As the time drew near for the ship to sail for Europe, the agents believed that the men on shore who were to receive the diamonds would reveal their anxiety. This proved to be a shrewd deduction. By a clever ruse the agents were able to intercept messages between the steward and the anxious men waiting in the hotel. The messages confirmed the report that the diamonds were still on the ship.

An hour before the S.S. *Assyria* was to sail, members of a special Customs racket squad went on board and began a thorough search. They found the diamonds. The steward was arrested and sent to prison.

One of the most interesting watch-smuggling cases involved a bonded Customs cartage firm and a clerk in the office of a customhouse broker.

Information was received by Customs agents in New York from informants in Frankfurt, Germany, that two cases containing valuable Swiss watch movements would arrive in the United States labeled "camera tripods," and valued by the shippers at only $200.

The two cases came into New York on the S.S. *Black Falcon* and were immediately spotted by Customs men. In this instance the agents resorted to the use of scientific instruments so that the smugglers would not know they had been discovered. With a device called an inspectoscope the agents were able to determine that the cases did, indeed, contain Swiss watch movements, instead of tripods, as the labels stated. The name and address of the person to whom the cases were to go were found to be fictitious. The agents patiently watched and waited for someone to claim the cases.

A few days later a sharp-eyed agent, who knew about the two cases of watches but had not been assigned to the investigation of them, spotted another case identical in size, shape, and wrapping on a truck that was leaving the Foreign Trade Zone of the New York waterfront. He followed the truck about the streets of the city until at last the driver delivered the case to the Appraiser's Stores. There it was opened and found to contain tripods. It was listed as one of four cases, all supposedly containing tripods, which were consigned to a company that did not exist.

The agents knew then that the smugglers were attempting the well-known "switch game." That is, they would try to switch decoy cases, which really did contain tripods of little value, for the cases containing the costly Swiss watch movements, on which a high duty had to be paid.

The suspicions of the agents were soon confirmed. The cases of watches were released with labels which stated that they contained only tripods and were to be sent on to Canada. A truck from the cartage company picked them up at the pier. It was followed by Customs agents in three radio-equipped cars. The driver was instructed to deliver the cases to bonded truckers, who were to take them on to Canada. But instead of taking them to the truckers, the cartman deposited them in the office of a Customs brokerage firm. There a clerk who was working with the smugglers was to switch the cases, sending the tripods on to Canada and the watch movements to his confederates in this country.

The Customs agents entered the office of the broker on the pretext of examining his license. They opened the cases and found the watches. They also found three cases containing camera equipment.

The plot to switch the cases was quickly established. On each of the cases containing tripods was an extra board, and on the boards were printed the same Customs serial numbers as those on the cases of watches. Once the cases had been switched, the tripods would have gone on to Canada, and the watches, valued at $37,529, would have remained in the United States without payment of duty. Four men who had participated in the scheme were arrested and sent to prison.

The practice of collecting customs on imports was carried on by the individual colonies before the Department of the Treasury was created. Each colony had different customs laws, and its own collector, whose task it was to levy duties on goods brought in from neighboring colonies. New York, New Jersey, and Connecticut, for example, levied heavy customs duties against the most humble of products. Peddlers from New Jersey were obliged to queue up at the New York Customs House to have eggs counted and chickens weighed. Connecticut firewood was taxed by adjoining colonies. Even cabbages and turnips taken from one state to another had to be appraised and import duties paid on them.

It was in the hope of ending this confusion and formulating sensible and just customs laws that the representatives of the thirteen colonies attending the Constitutional Convention in 1787 took up the problem in a thorough and thoughtful manner. They were successful in reaching an agreement, and when the Constitution was completed it provided that "The Congress shall have the power to lay and collect taxes, duties, imposts and excises . . . but all duties, imposts and excises shall be *uniform* throughout the United States."

The customs confusion was ended, and on July 31, 1789, the Fifth Act of Congress, signed by President Washington and Vice-President John Adams, established customs districts and ports of entry, and provided for the employment of customs officers and methods for the collecting of duties. The act was considered to be so beneficial and important that it was called by newspapers a "Second Declaration of Independence."

For many years the money collected by the Bureau of Customs was enough to pay all the costs of the Federal Government, excepting, of course, the costs of wars, for which the Government had to borrow money from Americans and foreign countries. Even as late as 1910, almost 60 per cent of the regular expenses of the Government were paid by customs duties on imports. Today they pay only slightly more than one per cent of the cost of government, but that is not a small sum. It amounts to about one and a half billion dollars.

Perhaps you may not realize how much customs affect your daily life. A moment's thought on the matter will bring an understanding. Just ask yourself how many things you use were made, at least in part, in a foreign country.

The clay used in making the dishes from which you eat may have come from England. The sugar you put on your cereal and fruit may have been grown in the Philippines. The cloth in your shirt or suit may have been woven in the British Isles or in some other European country. The coffee you drink certainly came from Latin or South America. Your tea came from the Orient. The mats on your table are probably a product of Japan; and your camera, your play sandals, and the pottery knickknacks and ornaments in your house may have come from the same nation. Your shoes may contain imported leather, your clothes may be colored with imported dyes, and the newsprint in your daily paper may have come to you from Scandinavian countries or from Canada. It is rather amazing how many articles that play commonplace parts in our lives come from beyond our borders.

The collection of customs, however, is not the only contribution the Bureau makes to the welfare and prosperity of the United States. Far from it.

It is against the law, for instance, to transport fissionable materials, except by special license, and the Customs agents co-operate with the Atomic Energy Commission in preventing traffic of this kind. It would be very difficult, if not impossible, for an enemy to smuggle an atomic weapon into the United States under the watchful and knowing eyes of Customs agents, who have scientific instruments such as Geiger counters available for their use.

The amazing work of Customs inspectors in aiding the Bureau of Narcotics, also a department of the Treasury, to suppress illegal dope traffic will be described in another chapter.

The Customs men stop gun smuggling, both into and out

of the country. They co-operate with the Department of Agriculture by halting the importation of seeds, fruits, animals, and birds that might spread human, plant, or animal diseases.

The Customs agents collect taxes due the Internal Revenue Bureau on imported merchandise. They assist the Bureau of the Mint by guarding against the illegal importation and exportation of gold, and see that imported gold does not get into improper channels. They gather trade statistics for the Bureau of the Census. They prevent the importation of goods which originated in Communist countries, such as Red China and North Korea, but which may have been shipped to the United States under false labels. They work closely with the Immigration Service to prevent aliens from entering or leaving this country in an illegal manner.

Through constant vigilance in the performance of their duties they assist invaluably in the detection and apprehension of criminals attempting to break numerous laws other than those of the Bureau of Customs. Not only smugglers are caught in the net spread about the four borders of the United States by Customs men, but also anarchists, counterfeiters, gangsters, and other undesirable persons, and swindlers of every conceivable breed.

Night and day, year in and year out the agents of the Bureau of Customs stand as a front line against the national and international underworlds.

III

YOUR MONEY AND MINE—PAPER MONEY

THE paper money of the United States is in several ways the best in the world. It is made of the finest materials obtainable. It is so cleverly designed and so well manufactured that it cannot successfully be counterfeited. But most important of all, it is "honest money." That is, its value is guaranteed by the Treasury's stocks of gold and silver, by other Federal assets, and by the unassailable integrity of the United States Government. These things make it the most valuable currency on earth, and it is sought after more than that of any other country.

Before the adoption of the Constitution, the individual colonies issued their own paper money. It was known as "Continental currency." In the long struggle with England, before and during the Revolution, when business conditions often were bad and colonial governments often were bankrupt, this currency frequently became worthless. These circumstances gave rise to a phrase that you may still hear today —"It's not worth a Continental."

It was not until 1785, several years after the guns of the Revolution were silent, that Congress adopted the dollar as the basic unit of American money and the decimal system as the method of reckoning. That is, a cent was .01 of a dollar, a dime was .10, a quarter was .25, and a half dollar was .50.

"What shall we use for money?" is a question older than recorded history. It is also a question as modern as today.

In ancient times, when men first began to buy and sell, what to use for money was a big problem. There had to be some standard of value on which transactions might be based.

In the time of Homer, oxen were measures of value. A suit of golden armor was worth a hundred oxen. That was nine hundred years before the birth of Christ. In ancient Crete, sheep were money, and the Jews of that period measured wealth in flocks and herds. The natives of the island of Yap, in the Pacific Ocean, even in comparatively recent times, used large stone wheels for money.

American Indians used shells, which were called wampum, until the colonists began to manufacture it in such great quantities and so cheaply that it lost its value. The Indians and the early fur traders used beaver skins as a standard of value; a beaver skin was worth so much per pound in British shillings, and merchandise of that value was given in exchange for it. For more than a hundred years tobacco was money in the colony of Virginia.

The Chinese were using paper money when Marco Polo visited their country in the thirteenth century. From him we know that Emperor Kubla Khan, as early as A.D. 1273, issued notes printed on mulberry paper. Each was stamped with the red seal of Kubla, and signed by his treasurers. The oldest paper money of which a piece is known to exist is the "Kwan" note, first issued in China in A.D. 1368. It is the size of a piece of typewriter paper.

Between the time of the signing of the Constitution and the Civil War, the Government did not itself issue paper money. Paper currency was used, but it was issued by banks chartered for the purpose by the Government.

It was in 1861, when the armies of the North and South were locked in terrible combat, that the Union Government issued the first Federal paper money. These were $5, $10, and $20 notes. During the next year the currency that was to give to our paper money the name "greenbacks" was placed in circulation in denominations of $1, $2, $5, $10, $20, $50, $100, $500, and $1,000.

Nothing larger than a $100 bill has been issued since 1945, but there are still in existence quite a number of $1,000, $5,000, and $10,000 bills—even a few $100,000 ones—that were previously issued.

The three types of paper currency now being printed are:

Federal Reserve notes, with green seal and numbers.

United States notes, with red seal and numbers.

Silver certificates, with blue seal and numbers.

Very few people have seen the old ornate $100, $1,000, $10,000, and $100,000 gold certificates, because they are issued only to Federal Reserve banks and are never put into general circulation. On each of them is printed: "This is to certify that there is on deposit in the Treasury of the United States of America (so many) dollars in gold, payable to bearer on demand as authorized by law." Only a Federal Reserve bank can make such a demand.

The silver certificates are backed up by silver dollars and silver bullion held by the Treasury.

The law requires that United States notes valued at $346,-681,016 be kept in circulation at all times. The Treasury keeps $156,039,430.93 worth of gold in reserve for these notes.

Special types of paper currencies were issued for emergency use during the last World War, and some of them are still in circulation. Now and then one drifts back to the Treasury, and it is destroyed. Among these special types were bills with brown seals and serial numbers. Another kind had the word HAWAII overprinted on its face and back.

Some were issued with gold seals and blue serial numbers. For the invasion of North Africa in 1942, bills bearing yellow seals and numbers were printed. These were the only money sent with American troops to that area at the time, and if the Germans had captured our paymasters, the bills would have been declared illegal tender and would have had no value.

On Fourteenth Street, near Washington's Tidal Basin, stand two large buildings that manufacture the most valuable and most wanted pieces of paper in the world. The buildings are the main plant of the Treasury's Bureau of Engraving and Printing, and their product is United States currency.

A visit to the Bureau, as thousands of people have discovered, is well worth while. The doors are open to callers, and each year more than 600,000 visitors to Washington are escorted through the various departments and workshops by well-trained guides.

It is a sight you would not be likely to forget. You would see greenbacks in neat million-dollar stacks, for about $30,000,000 worth of paper money is printed every day. It pours from the presses in a beautiful green flood; then it is thoroughly examined by experts for flaws, counted several times, packaged, and sent off to the Government's steady customers, the banks, for distribution to the public.

One of the most tiring questions asked by visitors is: "Where do we get samples?" It is asked hundreds of times each day, much to the boredom of Bureau workers. To them making money is just a job, like making shoes or tea kettles.

More $1 bills are printed, of course, than any other denomination, and in 1962 the Bureau produced about 1,132,000,000 of them. Next in public demand is the $5 note, and in the same period 262,920,000 were printed. But the $10 bill was not far behind the $5 bill in number, for 253,920,000 of them were issued. Strangely enough, fewer $50 bills were printed than $100 ones–6,048,000 compared with 6,480,000.

Altogether the number of pieces of new paper money issued in 1962 amounted to 1,781,132,000, and the face value of them was $8,202,564,000. The work cost the Government $9.06 for each thousand pieces.

The beginning of the Bureau of Engraving and Printing may be traced back to 1862, when 2 men and 4 women working in a single room in the Treasury Building attic began to put the seal of the Treasury on some $1 and $2 bills which had been printed by private banks. Today, the Bureau has more than 30 acres of floor space and employs 3,400 men and women.

With hundreds of visitors at one time moving through the pressrooms and other shops, you might gain the impression that the Bureau is somewhat careless about protecting its money. The impression would be false, for the Bureau is constantly suspicious and watchful. Not only are the visitors under the sharp eyes of uniformed guards, but persons in plain clothes patrol rooms and corridors at all times. The neat-looking young lady standing next to you may well have a .38 caliber pistol in her natty purse.

Despite all the precautions, money has been stolen from the Bureau on several occasions. Recently a Bureau janitor slipped through the security guards with two wrapped packages of $20 bills worth $160,000. However, all the thieves have been caught, and the janitor was no exception. He had not had time to eat his dinner at home that night before he was arrested.

While Bureau officials will not say that such a thing could not happen again, they will tell you that it is foolish to steal new money. The number of every new bill is recorded, and a missing one can be quickly traced.

The Bureau will show you money being printed and explain a great deal about the process, but there are some things it will not reveal. You may be told that the currency paper is made of 75 per cent cotton and 25 per cent linen, but no one can find out what materials go into the inks and dyes of the paper money. Those formulas are top secret. Equally well guarded is the process for manufacturing the fine paper containing the tiny red and blue threads, on which the money is printed. The paper comes from a heavily guarded mill in Massachusetts. So stringent are the laws protecting it that a person can be sent to jail for making any kind of paper with red and blue fibers in it—even though it be blank paper.

Every sheet of the special paper must be accounted for. If a sheet is found to be defective, it is canceled and sent to the auditing department. There the cancellation is verified, and the spoiled sheet is sent to another department to be destroyed under supervision of Treasury officers. Every step is checked and rechecked.

Paper that is used is counted twelve times from the moment it has been received at the Bureau until it is issued as finished currency.

Suppose a $5 bill is damaged while it is being made so that it cannot be put into circulation. It is removed and discarded through a system of checks and counterchecks, and it is replaced with a special kind of bill called a star note, which has a star in front of its serial number. Otherwise it is the same as the damaged bill. This is another means by which the Bureau keeps track of every serial number and every printed bill.

The dollar sign you use and which appears on our money is not new, nor was it invented in the United States. It is a product of evolution. For centuries the letters "P's" were used to indicate pesos, piastres, and pieces of eight. Gradually the small "s" came to be written over the "P," in a symbol similar to the $ mark. The symbol was widely used throughout the world before the adoption of the United States dollar in 1785.

If you should be lucky enough to acquire 233 new pieces of American paper money of any denomination, you would find that they make a stack exactly 1 inch high. Each piece of new currency is 2.61 inches wide and 6.14 inches long, and is .0043 of an inch in thickness.

Even if you don't look at the numbers in the corners of a bill, you can tell at once how much it is worth. Each denomination, from the $1 to the $100,000 bill, bears the same portrait on its front and the same picture or design on its back. Here they are:

DENOMINATION	FRONT	BACK
$1	Washington	Great Seal of the United States
$2	Jefferson	Monticello, Jefferson's Home
$5	Lincoln	Lincoln Memorial
$10	Hamilton	Treasury Building
$20	Jackson	White House
$50	Grant	Capitol
$100	Franklin	Independence Hall
$500	McKinley	Ornate 500
$1,000	Cleveland	Ornate 1,000
$5,000	Madison	Ornate 5,000
$10,000	Chase	Ornate 10,000
$100,000	Wilson	Ornate 100,000

Although producing paper money is by far the largest job of the Bureau, it has numerous other duties. It prints Government bonds, checks, officers' commissions, citations for heroes and patriots, postage stamps, revenue tax stamps, and even engraved invitations for White House social affairs.

Next to paper money, the $24,000,000 worth of postage stamps which the Bureau issues each year are of interest to the public, and especially to the millions of stamp collectors in every country of the earth.

Like United States currency, American postage stamps are the finest in the world. They have the same excellence in design, the same high quality of materials, and their value as unused stamps never varies.

The Bureau is not a stamp collector. It never holds stamps to let their value increase. As soon as the Bureau prints an issue of stamps, it turns them over to the Post Office Department for distribution to 36,000 post offices throughout the country.

There are now 54 different types of postage stamps being printed, in addition to commemorative stamps. They range from a value of half a cent to $5. The commemorative stamps are issued only on special occasions.

Just as United States money is always worth its face value, so are United States postage stamps. Any postage stamp ever issued by the United States can be used on mail, no matter how old it is. Of course old stamps, like old money, have increased value among collectors, simply because of their rarity. But to the Bureau one stamp or one bill is only worth as much as the amount stated on its face.

Every year the Treasury receives hundreds of letters from well-meaning people who believe they have discovered something new or strange on a paper bill. Some of the inquiries are repeated innumerable times, and they show that many people do examine their paper money with great care.

One of the questions often repeated is, "What is the make of the automobile on the $10 bill?" Some people ask whether it is a Ford, or a Chevrolet, or some older type of car. Patiently the Treasury replies that it is simply an auto, a composite, and does not represent any specific make.

When President Truman built a balcony on the White House, it was drawn into the picture of the mansion that appears on the $20 bill. The change was quickly noticed by many people, and they wrote to the Treasury about it. Some demanded to know why the change had been made, while others thought they might have come upon a unique bill, or perhaps a counterfeit one.

Frequently people think they see things in the design of

a bill that really are not there, such as numerals in the Lincoln Memorial shrubbery, or faces in the scrollwork.

Strangely enough, there is one "error" on all bills that bear the Great Seal of the United States, and it is unlikely that it will be corrected.

The legend on the seal is an abbreviation of the Latin: *Thesauri Americae Septentrionalis Sigillum.* Translated it means "The Seal of the Treasury of North America." Of course, to be accurate it should read "The Seal of the Treasury of the United States of America."

The seal, however, is older than the United States Government. The Continental Congress in 1778 appointed John Witherspoon, Gouverneur Morris, and Richard Henry Lee to design a Treasury seal. They carried out the task.

The seal approved by the Congress contained dots, which are the heraldic way of depicting gold. The thirteen stars on the bend of the shield were for the thirteen original colonies. The scales represented those held by the blind goddess, Justice. It bore a key, commonly used in heraldry to denote offices of state.

When the United States Government was established in 1789, the Continental seal was continued in use. It has been in use ever since.

IV

YOUR MONEY AND MINE—HARD MONEY

No MONEY is more valuable than the hard money of the United States. The coins of some nations contain alloys that decrease their intrinsic value. Those of the United States are exactly what they are purported to be. That is, without exception, they contain certain amounts of valuable metals, and the amounts are never changed by the Treasury in secret. The world can depend upon their quality.

The first coiners of gold and silver known to history were the Lydians, in Asia Minor. The name of their king, Croesus, became a synonym for great wealth. Coinage was learned by the Greeks from the Lydians, and the art was taken from Greece to Rome.

Metals were used for money in Egypt as early as 2,500 years before the birth of Christ. In the Bible (Genesis 23:16) is the passage: "Abraham weighed unto Ephron 400 shekels of silver, current money with the merchant." It was to pay for a burial place for Abraham's family. Babylonian records show that about 550 B.C. some temples were also banks, that they took in money on deposit and lent it with interest.

During the early days of our nation, various foreign coins, chiefly English, French, and Spanish, were in circulation along the eastern seaboard. They not only varied in their intrinsic value, but were affected by the good and bad fortunes of their governments. On one day American traders and businessmen might favor Spanish money more than British or French, and on another day the situation might be quite the reverse. As a result there was frequent confusion and commerce was interrupted.

Plans for the capital city of Washington had not yet been drawn when the United States Government established our monetary system and ordered the first coins to be made. These first coins were called half dimes, and they were minted in Philadelphia from household silver sent from Mount Vernon, Washington's plantation on the bank of the Potomac River in Virginia. The half dimes were not put into circulation. Congress presented them to President Washington, and he gave them to his friends as souvenirs.

Soon thereafter United States coins were being made from gold, silver, and copper. There were gold eagles valued at $10, and half eagles and quarter eagles. The silver coins were dollars, half dollars, quarters, dimes, and half dimes. Cents and half cents were made of copper.

After 1851 a three-cent piece was minted from copper at various times, and in 1875 a twenty-cent coin was issued. Between 1864 and 1873 a two-cent piece was in circulation. The nickel was introduced in 1866. During World War II a zinc-coated steel cent was coined as a wartime metal-saving measure, and a "nickel" made of silver, copper, and manganese—no nickel, which was needed for the war effort—was put into circulation.

The act passed by Congress in 1792 which authorized the first coining of American money also created the Bureau of the Mint, which is a part of the Treasury Department. The first mint was located in Philadelphia, then the capital of the United States. It is still operating. Later other branches of the Bureau of the Mint were established in Denver; San

Francisco; New York; Fort Knox, Kentucky; and West Point, New York.

Only the mints at Philadelphia and Denver produce coins now. They turn out a silver, copper, and nickel flood each working day. The New York and San Francisco branches are now chiefly assay offices.

More pennies are made, of course, than any other coin. In a recent year about 2,000,000,000 of them were produced. The annual production of half dollars, quarters, and dimes amounts to about 500,000,000. Each year between 200,000,000 and 225,000,000 new nickels are made.

In addition to making and distributing all coins, the Mint has numerous duties. It guards the Government's stores of gold and silver bullion. It issues licenses to persons who need these precious metals in industry and business, such as jewelry manufacturers, doctors, and artists. It refines gold and silver from ores. It makes coins on order for several foreign nations, and it assays samples of precious metals sent to it by mines and prospectors.

Only the Bureau of the Mint can distribute the coins it makes, and it has only 37 customers. These are the 12 Federal Reserve banks of the United States, their 24 branches, and the Treasurer of the United States. It is through the Federal Reserve that the hard money reaches the banks, which transact business directly with the public, the millions of depositors and individual customers, from gigantic corporations like General Motors and Standard Oil to the small shopkeeper and the office worker.

One thing that many people do not realize is that hard money is governed as much by the law of supply and demand as are the products it buys. For instance, when business conditions are poor, less money is in circulation and the Mint is not required to coin as much as it is when business conditions are good. Here is an example: In the depression year of 1932, the Mint produced only 19,000,000 coins, but in 1959 it produced 2,500,000,000.

The daily production of coins is governed in many strange ways, and the distribution of them is affected by incidents one might think would have nothing to do with the business of the Mint. Suppose a company that makes breakfast cereal launches a nation-wide advertising campaign. For a box top and a penny boys and girls can obtain a toy of some sort. Such a promotion scheme may result in as many as 50,000,000 pennies flooding into the town where the cereal is made. Distribution in the area is upset. The town has millions more pennies than it can use, and the Mint has to get busy and remove them.

If a state permits the installation of large numbers of new vending machines, it follows that more coins will be needed in that area, and the Mint has to see that they get there. If a city imposes a new tax on cigarettes, more pennies will be quickly needed in it. Recently one city did increase its tax on cigarettes, and the demand for pennies suddenly became so great that the Mint had to send 30 of its trucks, each carrying $43,000 worth of pennies weighing 15 tons, to relieve the situation there.

Some of the demands for money are mysterious and cannot be explained. New Yorkers seem to hoard half dollars, but no one can say why. On the other hand, Boston people do not seem to care for half dollars, and they quickly dispose of them.

In some sections of Maryland bank tellers never seemed to be able to keep enough nickels on hand, and the Mint didn't know the reason. The mystery was solved when a Mint official happened to be traveling in Maryland. He began to play a nickel slot machine, and after he had lost several dollars, it suddenly occurred to him why Maryland banks suffered from nickel shortages.

No silver dollars have been made since 1935. Americans

dislike them because of their weight—all except Americans in Nevada. Everyone there loves them, for they are used in gambling and for slot machines which advertise jackpots of $500, but seldom pay off that much to the player. Many silver dollars disappear from Nevada gambling casinos, for thousands of visitors take them home as souvenirs. Most of these eventually are spent and reach Federal Reserve banks, which send them back to Nevada, where the demand for them is constant.

An interesting sideline of the Mint is the striking (making) of military medals, such as the Congressional Medal of Honor. The Mint also strikes a medallion for each new President. Anyone can buy all 35 of these medallions for $3 a piece.

New modern machinery enables the Mint to produce more money with only a quarter of the employees needed a few years ago, and at greatly reduced cost. The first step in coinage operations is to prepare the alloy. In the case of silver coins, the alloy consists of 100 parts of copper and 900 parts of silver. The alloy is melted in electric induction furnaces and poured into molds to form ingots, which are in the form of thin bars.

Next the ingots are put through rolling mills and reduced to strips of the thickness required for the particular coin to be made. The strips are then fed into cutting presses. The presses cut circular blanks of the approximate dimensions of the finished coins, after which the blanks are softened in annealing furnaces. Then the blanks are washed in chemical solutions which burnish the metal.

The most important operation comes when the blanks are placed in the stamping or coining machine. Each blank is held firmly by a collar as it is struck under great pressure. Pennies and dimes require a pressure of 40 tons, but the pressure used on silver dollars amounts to 170 tons. Upper and lower dies impress the design on both sides of the coin at the same time. What is called "reeding"—grooves on the rim of the coin—makes it impossible for it to be shaved without detection.

Scraps of metal remaining after the blank coins are cut from the strips are resmelted. Despite the great care taken to safeguard every bit of the precious metal dust, some temporarily eludes the coiners. When the old San Francisco Mint stopped making coins, the building was torn apart, and gold dust valued at $175,000 was recovered.

The Treasury states clearly the kinds and amounts of metal in today's coins. Here they are:

Kind of Coin	Metal Content (Grains)		Gross Weight (Grains)
	Silver	*Copper*	
Dollar	371.25	41.25	412.50
Half Dollar	173.61	19.29	192.90
Quarter	86.805	9.645	96.45
Dime	34.722	3.858	38.58
	Copper	*Nickel*	
Nickel	57.87	19.29	77.16
	Copper	*Zinc and Tin*	
Penny	45.60	2.40	48.00

In guarding the gold and silver bullion reserves of the Government, the Bureau of the Mint exercises extraordinary care.

The main depository for gold is at Fort Knox, Kentucky. It was built in 1936, cost $560,000, and is the safest on earth. At present its vault contains gold bullion valued at $12,483,-414,764.

The great vault is built on two levels, and is divided into compartments. The door to it weighs more than twenty tons, and no one person knows all the combinations to it. When it is to be opened, several persons must dial separate combinations, and each person knows only one of them. The vault casing is constructed of steel plates, steel I-beams, and steel cylinders with hoop bands and encased in concrete. The outer wall of the depository is made of 16,500 cubic feet of granite, 4,200 cubic yards of concrete, 750 tons of reinforcing steel, and 670 tons of structural steel.

The Mint buys gold at $35 an ounce, the price set by law. Gold coins are no longer issued to the public, and the hoarding of gold is prohibited. But the gold dollar is still the standard unit of value of the United States, although we are not now operating on the gold standard we knew prior to 1933. The present system is known as a "gold bullion standard."

The Secretary of the Treasury is authorized to buy newly mined silver, both at home and abroad, as he believes the country requires it.

Silver bullion owned by the United States is stored chiefly in the Mint's depository at West Point, New York. More than 32,000 tons of it are kept in the 23 compartments of its vault. Each compartment measures approximately 20x45 feet. Their total capacity is two billion ounces, or about 70,000 tons.

The silver depository, which is the largest in the world, cost more than $500,000 to build. It was first occupied in 1938.

The building is rectangular, windowless, one story in height, and measures 170 x 256 feet. Offices and guard rooms are on the first floor and mezzanine, and light and air for them is obtained through skylights. The remainder of the structure is under a solid composition roof. A vertical-lift steel door at the front permits the entrance and departure of bullion trucks. When this door is closed, loading and unloading operations are completely isolated. To the rear of the loading platform are rolling steel doors and checking rooms, through which the storage vault is reached. The master vault door is equipped with a time lock, and it is made of drill-proof and flame-proof metal.

A fence nine feet in height surrounds the entire building. It has a steel gate that is controlled by guards who regulate the entrance and departure of all persons and vehicles. An inside corridor connects the turret watchtowers at the four corners of the building. Sentries can observe the terrain in all directions.

A coin lasts from two to three decades, its lifetime governed, of course, by the extent of its usage. Banks send worn coins back to the Mint in old sacks. After the coins have been counted, the full sacks are held over fires. The bottoms are burned away and the coins fall through, to be melted and molded into ingots.

The story is told of how one workman in the shop tried to steal some of the old coins, many of which were still passable. He sewed a hidden pocket into his coat, and each day he would fill it with half dollars that were about to be destroyed. In time, fellow employees became aware that he was using old money to pay for his lunches and the things he purchased in shops. They became suspicious of him and he was arrested. His hoard of worn-out half dollars was found. What he had forgotten was that Mint employees are paid in bright, shiny, new money.

The words "In God We Trust" have not always been printed on United States coins. They were first used on a two-cent piece in 1864. During the Civil War religious sentiment greatly increased in the states of the Union, and Salmon P. Chase, then Secretary of the Treasury, received a number of appeals from devout persons urging that the Deity be recognized on our money, as He was on the money of other nations.

Secretary Chase agreed with this sentiment, and he wrote the director of the Mint requesting that a suitable motto be inscribed on our coins. "No nation," said Chase, "can be strong except in the strength of God, or safe except in His defense."

After the two-cent piece, the motto "In God We Trust" next appeared on both gold and silver coins in 1866. The nickel five-cent piece carried it from 1866 to 1883, when it was dropped. It was not restored until the introduction of the Jefferson nickel in 1938. The penny first carried it in 1909, and the dime in 1916. A law was passed by Congress in 1955 requiring that the motto be printed on all money of the United States.

Most nations adopted an official motto early in their history, but it was not until 1956, more than a century and a half after the signing of the Constitution, that the United States adopted one. In that year President Dwight D. Eisenhower signed a Congressional resolution which made "In God We Trust" our official national motto.

Numerous persons—senators, congressmen, Presidents and Cabinet officers—have been called "watch dog of the Treasury." But Nero, a real dog, has a better claim to the title than any man.

Henry Voight, chief coiner of the first United States Mint, at Philadelphia, was Nero's sponsor. He persuaded the Mint to buy Nero for $3. You can see a handwritten record of the transaction in one of the Mint's old ledgers. It tells of the expenditure of $3 "for a Dog for the yard." Over the course of several years are other entries showing payments for food and licenses for Nero.

In those early years a night watchman was required to visit all sections of the Mint every hour. Nero went with him. To prevent Nero from becoming friendly with others, no one was permitted to feed him except the night watchman. The story is told of how one night the watchman, for an unexplained reason, failed to make his customary rounds. But the money of the Mint was safe, for Nero dutifully made the rounds all by himself.

The same early records which tell about Nero also speak of "rum allowances" and "drink money" paid to Mint employees. These payments ranged from $1 to $3 a month. If the employee didn't care to drink, the allowance was added to his pay check.

Watchdogs of the Treasury like Nero were used for some years, but the Mint stopped giving its employees money for drinks early in the nineteenth century.

V

COUNTERFEITERS AND FORGERS

ON A HOT July day in 1865 a tall man stood with his right hand raised before the Secretary of the Treasury, Hugh McCulloch, and took an oath.

"I will faithfully discharge the duties upon which I am about to enter," he said in a low, clear voice. "So help me God."

The tall man was William P. Wood, a former prison warden, and he had just been appointed the first chief of the new United States Secret Service.

The Government created the Secret Service for reasons of dire necessity. During the Civil War, which had just ended, more than a third of the paper money in circulation was counterfeit. All during the great conflict, counterfeiters —called "boodlers" in those days—had made worthless greenbacks in frightening quantities. There was no national police force to combat them, and local authorities were helpless to halt the flood of imitation currency.

Unless the counterfeiting could be stopped, the public would lose all confidence in the nation's money, and the economy of the country would collapse. It was the job of William P. Wood, with a handful of assistants, to restore and maintain that public confidence. There was only one way it could be done, and that was by catching and imprisoning the persons who were endangering the nation's commerce—the counterfeiters.

They did the job. Scores of counterfeiting plants were uncovered and destroyed, and the operators were arrested, convicted, and sent to jail. Respect for the new crime-fighting organization grew swiftly, not only among criminals but among numerous foreign governments, and ever since then the Secret Service has been admired and honored throughout the world.

The crime of counterfeiting is one of the oldest criminal activities. It is believed by historians that the Emperor Nero was the first coin counterfeiter, although many European rulers of the ancient past were known to have debased the money of their own countries, and it is possible that Nero was merely following a custom which had originated before his time.

After the Pilgrims had settled in Massachusetts, it was not long before they began to make counterfeit wampum to fleece the Indians. During the Revolutionary War, the British dumped so many tons of counterfeit money into the colonies that the Continental currency soon became worthless.

The value of counterfeiting as a weapon of war is well documented throughout history. It has been used extensively and successfully as a silent saboteur. Perhaps the chaos created by the counterfeiting of the Continental currency during the American Revolution set the pattern for the disruption of the assignat currency issued by the French Revolutionary Government in 1789.* Enemies of the Revolution promptly began to counterfeit the new money, and by 1796 had placed some fifteen billion counterfeit francs in circula-

* Assignats were notes issued as currency and supported by the value of French lands which had been appropriated by the state.

tion. The result was that the assignat became worthless, and it was finally repudiated by the French Government.

In 1812, Emperor Napoleon Bonaparte established an elaborate counterfeiting plant in Paris. He used the money it produced to buy military supplies for his invasion of Russia.

Closer to our own time was the wholesale counterfeiting of foreign currencies by Adolf Hitler. The Nazi dictator combed Germany to find expert engravers, printers, and other technicians. They were taken to a special compound at one of the concentration camps, and they were ordered to make counterfeit passports, identification cards, and other documents, but their main task soon became the production of counterfeit money.

American troops captured German trucks loaded with huge crates of counterfeit British banknotes that were so well made they defied detection except by experts. Secret Service agents were sent to Europe to cooperate with military authorities in piecing together the amazing story of this attempt by the Nazis to crumble the economic structure of their enemies. It was found that large amounts of counterfeit British money already had been distributed in England. To prevent further disturbances of its currency, the British Government completely redesigned its pound notes.

Secret Service agents also learned that the Nazis had tried in vain to duplicate the paper money of the United States. After the war, Hermann Goering admitted: "It was too good for us." This was an outstanding illustration of the mastery achieved by Treasury Department engravers.

It is a high tribute to the effective work of the Secret Service that practically all Americans today accept and pay out money without stopping to think that it may be counterfeit. While the Secret Service greatly appreciates the compliments it receives, it feels duty bound to warn people repeatedly that failure to make any examination of the money that passes through their hands can result in serious financial losses, if not disaster. Overconfidence and carelessness on the part of the public are two of the counterfeiter's greatest assets, and many people become victims simply because they pay so little attention to their money.

The trust the people have in our money is, of course, another tribute to the highly skilled technicians who make it. A famous designer once complained that American paper money was bad art. Perhaps it is, but the men who engrave it are not disturbed. They are not interested in creating artistic bills, but bills that cannot be imitated. The doodles and ornaments they scratch into steel printing plates are put there for only one purpose, and that is to defeat counterfeiters.

In engraving a new design for a bill, no one engraver does all the work. Each man assigned to the task is a specialist. One works only on portraits, another on lettering, another on scroll work, vignettes, and ornamentation. Each engraver, with a steel tool known as a graver, and aided by a powerful magnifying glass, carefully carves his portion of the design into the plate. He knows that one false cut, a slip of his tool, or one miscalculation of the width or the depth of a line, may destroy the merit of his work. A single mistake can mean that weeks, or even months, of labor will have been wasted. Specimens of the work of Treasury engravers have been awarded the highest premiums at all world's fairs and exhibitions since 1872. In all the thousands of attempts that have been made, no counterfeiter has ever been able to duplicate the products of the Bureau of Engraving and Printing.

Yet, they keep on trying to do it by scores each year.

After World War II counterfeiting increased with unprecedented rapidity. During the war, when food, gasoline and other commodities were being rationed, criminals manufactured millions of counterfeit ration coupons. With the coming of peace and the end of rationing, many of these criminals turned to the production of counterfeit money. Millions of dollars worth of "homemade" American currency began to appear both in the United States and in foreign countries.

The stability of the United States dollar made it highly desirable throughout the world during the first years of the postwar period. For the first time in history, the protection of our currency became a serious worldwide problem. The Secret Service, working in close relationship with honorable foreign governments, launched a war against counterfeiters on an international scale.

In 1947, Secret Service agents and French detectives captured eleven counterfeiters and more than two million dollars in counterfeit $10 bills which had been produced in an isolated farmhouse near Marseilles. The French police also cracked down on other gangs, and by 1952 the counterfeiting of American money in France had been greatly reduced. Similar successes were achieved by the Secret Service in cooperation with the authorities in England, Germany, Italy, Belgium, and Switzerland. British agents also rendered excellent assistance to the Secret Service in Hong Kong. There concerted enforcement efforts stamped out extensive counterfeiting enterprises which were responsible for the manufacture and circulation of some of the best counterfeit $20, $50, and $100 bills ever produced.

A recent Secret Service report shows the extent to which American money has been counterfeited since the end of the last World War. The list on the following page includes both bills and coins.

Not long ago, in Los Angeles, agents arrested a leading actor during the performance of a play, *Charley's Aunt*, and seized a quantity of counterfeit bills when he attempted to hide them under the stage floor. Several of the actor's accomplices were arrested in other cities, and nearly half a million dollars' worth of bogus bills was seized from this ring. The

Fiscal Year	Amount Passed on the Public	Amount Captured Before it Could be Circulated	Total Seizures
1946	$ 48,400.87	$ 25,862.20	$ 74,263.07
1947	70,328.09	185,062.95	255,391.04
1948	145,214.91	2,949,015.10	3,094,230.01
1949	338,062.84	619,700.87	957,763.71
1950	735,127.06	554,154.20	1,289,281.26
1951	521,187.68	918,249.15	1,439,436.83
1952	379,861.99	394,068.95	773,930.94
1953	178,384.49	115,737.37	294,121.86
1954	145,933.71	209,365.61	355,299.32
1955	107,457.32	919,721.75	1,027,179.07
1956	73,041.34	445,044.82	518,086.16
1957	107,295.21	1,446,704.04	1,553,999.25
1958	142,622.26	568,670.60	711,292.86

actor may have been very good in playing the part of an "aunt," but he was a failure in his relations with an "uncle" —Uncle Sam.

Most counterfeiters are clumsy. They bungle their work and display extraordinary stupidity. One even counterfeited half dollars that contained more silver than the genuine. Every time he passed one, he lost money. The Secret Service caught him, and his valuable half dollars are among its most treasured souvenirs.

Some counterfeiters have gone to the trouble of making imitation pennies, although the Secret Service does not understand why. No one could get rich passing counterfeit pennies.

In 1957 an engineer counterfeited a large quantity of nickels. He posed as the owner of vending machines, which he thought would explain why he had so many nickels, and he deposited $5,000 worth in several banks. The agents were soon on his trail, and when the public was warned to watch out for the imitation nickels, the counterfeiter threw his dies and other equipment into a river. The agents could not find the man's vending machines, because there were none, but they had his bad nickels, and after Navy divers found the counterfeit dies for the coins in the river, the agents soon had the lawbreaker himself.

The Secret Service never abandons a trail until its end is reached. In one recent case they searched for a counterfeiter for ten years. They knew who he was, for they had arrested him before and they were familiar with the peculiarities of his work. Cities and towns were ceaselessly scoured for him, and at last he was found operating a Chicago photographic studio under an assumed name. The plates and counterfeiting paraphernalia with which he turned out his bogus money were found in the studio.

Counterfeiters are like weeds—new ones keep springing up as fast as old ones are mowed down. Yet, the Secret Service keeps up with them.

The arrest of a Camden, New Jersey, man for passing $10 counterfeit bills led to the apprehension of two others, one of whom confessed that he had thrown several counterfeit plates into a sewer. Agents were able to recover 23 of the plates, and these led to a printer. He, too, was taken into custody, and a quantity of bogus $1 and $5 bills was discovered in the printing shop. This bonus was something the agents had not expected when they caught the first man.

Last year a young man in his teens was arrested in Wichita, Kansas, for making and attempting to pass counterfeit $20 bills. The young man was a good amateur photographer, but he had much to learn about counterfeiting. While he was working in an offset printing plant, he learned how to make plates—or thought he did—and he returned to the plant after hours to experiment in the production of counterfeit money.

He printed $10,000 worth which he thought quite good, and he stored it in a locker in a bus depot.

Soon after he spent the first bill—in a grocery store—the clerk discovered that it was counterfeit. He pursued the young man, who apologized and gave the clerk good money for the bad. Then the ambitious youthful counterfeiter tried again in another store, but again a clerk discovered that the bill was bogus. The young man fled. Secret Service agents were soon on his trail, and he was arrested. Plates and counterfeit money were uncovered in his home. A thumbprint found on one of the bills led the agents to another young man of sixteen, who confessed he had been an accomplice in the attempt to swindle Wichita merchants. Both young men went to prison.

Counterfeiters turn up in the most unexpected places. One operation was uncovered in an Alabama prison. There three inmates had conspired to print false $5 bills. They kept the plates hidden in a metal electric cable box, and the negatives were found in an old almanac. Needless to say, the three men remained in prison.

In Las Vegas, Nevada, a practicing psychologist was arrested for stealing an expensive camera. Then it was discovered that he had been using it in the manufacture of counterfeit $20 and $50 bills, some of which had turned up in the Las Vegas gambling casinos. In prison the psychologist was launched on a less scientific profession, that of washing clothes in the prison laundry.

A short time ago two men were arrested in Phoenix, Arizona, for conspiring to produce a million dollars' worth of counterfeit $10 and $20 bills. When their hidden workshop was searched, Secret Service agents learned that the men had even greater ambitions. Plates were found for $500 and $1,000 bills. How the men expected to dispose of such large bills was not explained. It would have been impossible through banks, and few stores or hotels will accept bills of such large denomination without having them examined by an expert, such as a bank teller.

For a long time the astute Secret Service agents had expected to find a traveling counterfeit plant, and at last they did. It was located in a house trailer at May's Landing, New Jersey. The counterfeiter was caught while busy at work on an offset press.

The Secret Service has a list of more than 800 crooked schemes used by clever swindlers to trick unsuspecting Americans out of their money. One of the most notorious of these is called the "Green Goods Game" (GGG). It has been exposed countless times, and the public has been warned repeatedly to watch out for it, yet it is still one of the most successful frauds employed by confidence men.

The GGG swindler has equipment which he claims can duplicate genuine currency. This equipment generally consists of a fancy wooden or metal box studded with dials and knobs and little electric lights, all intended to impress and mystify the victim.

When the GGG man has enticed an unwary person into his den, he proceeds to demonstrate how the box can reproduce paper money. He puts a good $10 bill into a small compartment of the box with a piece of plain paper of the same size, and closes the lid. The process of duplicating the good bill, he tells his victim, is done with a "secret chemical" known only to him. Then he presses a switch. Lights flash and there is a buzzing noise. In a few minutes he opens the compartment lid, and there before the amazed eyes of his audience are two perfectly good $10 bills.

The victim is permitted to take the two bills to a bank for examination, if he wishes to do so, and if he does, he finds that both of them are genuine. Thus he is convinced. He either buys the machine for a fabulous sum or he delivers to the swindler a large quantity of good paper money to be "duplicated." In either case, that is the last he ever sees of both the swindler and his money.

The secret of the GGG game is simple. Before the demonstration of the machine, the swindler secretes two good bills in a hidden section of the compartment. By turning the dials, he slides the hidden compartment into the place formerly occupied by the one good bill and the piece of white paper. When the compartment is reopened, there are the two good bills. The other good bill and the white paper are merely out of sight.

Counterfeiting's companion crime is forgery. A police detective once remarked that where you find a counterfeiter you find either a potential or a veteran forger of Government checks. The two breeds have much in common in addition to the fact that they are both criminals. Their common goal is the swindling of the public with fraudulent Federal paper, be that paper in the form of currency, bonds, Government travel orders, Treasury notes, postage stamps, coins, or checks.

For this reason the law makes forgers as much the game of Secret Service agents as counterfeiters are. And thereby hang a thousand tales.

Checks have been used in some form for centuries. Many years ago, in the Middle Ages, when a man went to a bank to deposit some money, the banker would cut notches in a stick. Then he would split the stick in half. The bank kept one piece and gave the other to the depositor as his receipt. The piece held by the bank was known as the "check." The one held by the depositor was called the "bank stock."

When the depositor wanted to draw some money out of the bank, he brought in his half of the stick. It would be matched with the "check" held by the bank. If the notches fitted, the depositor got his money. If the notches did not match, the bank would not make payment. The procedure was known as "tallying," and it is derived from the French word *tailler*, meaning "to cut." This is the origin of the word "teller" as we know it today.

Strangely enough, the word "check," as we use it in banking and finance, comes from the French *eschequier*, meaning "chessboard." This is the equivalent of the English "exchequer." If you are familiar with the game of chess, you know that the king is the only piece that may be held in "check," which means that the king is under the control of his opponent. Originally the British "cheque" meant the stub of a draft or other form of bank order, on which a brief description of the transaction was written, much the same as the stubs in our checkbooks of today. This description served not only as a record of the draft, but also represented a control, or "check," against it. Here, in another form, was the idea of the notched and split stick used in the Middle Ages.

The sad truth is that of the 350,000,000 checks issued each year by the Government, thousands fail to reach their rightful owners, and the reasons for this are chiefly two in number: Carelessness on the part of the public, and the activities of forgers.

The Secret Service receives about 2,500 cases of check forgery to investigate every month. Let us examine a few of the Service's reports which dramatically illustrate why there are so many. The following incidents are from Service files:

A woman walked into a furniture store in a Midwestern city and began shopping for some new bedroom furniture. As she sat on a bed and bounced up and down gently to test the mattress, an enthusiastic young salesman approached. He escorted the customer from one bedroom suite to another, giving her a smooth patter about the merits of each. Obviously the lady was not "just looking"—she was going to buy, and the salesman became more and more anxious to clinch the deal. Finally the woman decided on a set, but she hesitated when the salesman brought out his sales book.

"I don't have enough cash for a down payment," she explained, "but I do have my Government pension check, and if you could cash that for me—?"

The salesman was all smiles. "Of course, ma'am. A Government check is as good as gold, isn't it? How much is it for?"

She took the check out of her purse. "It's for $120," she said. "Do you think you could take out a down payment of $30 and give me the rest in cash?"

"Why not?" the salesman said. "You just endorse it and I'll do the rest."

She turned away and leaned over a small table as though she were writing on the check. A moment later she handed it to the salesman. He tossed it in his cash register and gave her $90 in cash and a receipt for her down payment. She walked out of the store.

The next morning, when the store's cashier prepared the previous day's receipts to be deposited in the bank, she found the Government check. She turned it over to make sure it was properly endorsed, and received a shock.

The name of the person to whom the check had been made out was written on the back, but someone had already discovered that the endorsement was a forgery, had drawn two lines through it, and had written underneath it: "No good—this check was stolen."

How the woman who bought the bedroom suite obtained possession of the check was not known. But if the young salesman had even glanced at the endorsement, he would not have cashed it. A forged Government check is just as worthless as any bad personal check, and the person who cashes it is the loser.

Carelessness on the part of merchants and businessmen has resulted in countless losses to them.

When he was arrested in Miami, Florida, not long ago, Norman Joseph Huber angrily asked a Secret Service agent: "Why pick on me when there are counterfeiters to catch?"

The Secret Service had good reasons for picking on Huber. They had wanted to catch up with him for some time. Huber was a fabulous forger, thief, and burglar who had victimized people in all parts of the United States and Canada. At the time he was taken into custody on a charge of forging Government checks, he had a suitcase full of identification papers, including drivers' licenses, Social Security cards, and credit cards. This dapper ex-convict stole 300 blank money orders from a Post Office in Tonawanda, New York, which he had filled out and cashed along the eastern seaboard. He had pilfered bank books from the mail, and by using them he had fraudulently withdrawn $11,415.89 from banks. He had burglarized homes and had stolen stocks, bonds, jewelry, and furs of great value. He had one weakness which had helped agents to track him down–dog and horse races. They caught him while he was spending his stolen money at Florida race tracks.

One day a compensation check for $7,143 was mailed from Washington to Joseph D. Martin at 707 West Fifth Street, Dayton, Ohio. Martin didn't live there. His home was at 907 West Fifth Street. A Government clerk had made a mistake in the address, and thereby launched a complicated forgery case that took the Secret Service agents some time to solve.

During the next three months five more compensation checks totaling $1,240.90 were mailed to Martin at the same wrong address. It was the home of Odell and Gladys Andrews, who concocted a scheme for cashing them and stealing the money.

The Andrews couple did not attempt at once to cash the larger check. They held it for several months, but during that time they cashed four of the smaller ones. This they accomplished in a rather unusual way. They made what was purported to be Joseph Martin's "mark" on the back of each check. A mark, such as an X or some other symbol, can be used by a person who cannot write. Thus they made Martin out to be illiterate. Underneath his "mark" they boldly wrote their own names and address to indicate that they had witnessed Martin place his "X" on the checks. A food market and a bank in Dayton cashed the checks.

Shortly afterward the couple put Martin's "mark" on a large check for $822.90 sent to him by the Government; then they signed their own names on it and presented it to Al Wilson, the credit manager of Ray's Department Store in Dayton. They told Wilson they were buying some things for Martin and wanted the balance in cash for him. Their purchases took only a small part of the check and Wilson gave them the balance in cash.

Next, Odell and Gladys Andrews went to Covington, Kentucky, to talk with Harrison Stewart, an elderly friend. They still had the big check for $7,143. Stewart could neither read nor write. The Andrews persuaded him to go back to Dayton with them and pose as Joseph D. Martin, promising to give him $1,000.

Once more they went to see kindly Al Wilson in Ray's Department Store, taking Stewart with them. Stewart was introduced to Wilson as Martin, and the Andrews couple told Wilson that Stewart wanted to make some extensive purchases. Before that could be done, however, the large check would have to be cashed. They didn't ask Wilson to cash it, but they did ask him to go with them to a nearby bank and identify "Martin." Thinking he was in line for a good sale, Wilson agreed. At the bank Stewart placed his fraudulent "X" on the check as the purported signature of Martin. Wilson acted as a witness, and a bank officer cashed the check.

Odell and Gladys Andrews gave their friend Stewart only $100, and they fled with the balance of the money in a new automobile.

One evening Secret Service agents walked into their room

in Cincinnati and took them into custody. It had been a peculiar trail, but the agents had never lost it.

One of the biggest forgery cases on record involved a man who made his residence in the remote little city of Belle Fourche, South Dakota. The agents had trailed him through forty-eight states, Canada, and Mexico, but always they were a step or two behind. In two years this man had cashed more than $50,000 worth of forged checks of all types. Suddenly the unceasing vigilance and bulldog persistence of the agents brought them their reward. The man was caught in the act of trying to cash a counterfeit Treasury check in a Denver supermarket. When the agents searched his apartment in Belle Fourche, they found 89 fraudulent Treasury Department checks, several hundred commercial checks, a printing press, and other equipment used by professional forgers. The man was sentenced to serve 88 years in prison.

Not all merchants are as gullible as Al Wilson was–indeed, as thousands of other "Al Wilsons" are in all sections of the country. Some take precautions before they cash Treasury checks, as the Secret Service shows in the following illustration:

Peter Grant was a druggist. One day a stranger walked into his store and asked him to cash a Treasury check for $40 which was made out to Charles Jones, 151 Elm Street.

Grant took the check, and said: "Oh, you're Charles Jones, eh? Are you by any chance Frank Jones's brother?"

The stranger replied cautiously: "Well, I–uh–no. No, that must be a different Charlie Jones."

"I see," the druggist said. "But I see you live at 115 Elm Street. (The address on the check was 151 Elm Street.) That's right next door to the new school they're building, isn't it?" (The druggist knew there was no new school being constructed on Elm Street.)

"Uh–yes, it is," replied the stranger. "Right next door."

"Okay," the druggist said. "I don't have enough money

in the register. I'll get it from the safe. Just excuse me a minute."

The druggist went into the rear and quickly telephoned the police. A squad car was at his door in three minutes, and the stranger was arrested for attempting to cash a stolen Government check.

To such sharp merchants as Peter Grant the Secret Service agents doff their hats.

Yet, in spite of educational campaigns carried on from coast to coast by the Secret Service, in spite of countless warnings, the carelessness continues. In Secret Service files are cases in which twelve-year-old boys have stolen and cashed Government checks marked "Old Age and Survivors Insurance."

In New York City recently the manager of a chain grocery store cashed a negative photostatic copy of a Government check.

Innumerable times, when forgers have stolen Treasury checks, they have taken *all* mail from the box and have used it to identify themselves to merchants. Scores of captured forgers have told the Secret Service that in most cases they were not asked for any identification at all by the persons who cashed stolen checks for them. In other cases, forgers have identified themselves with cheap printed identification cards which come as samples in new wallets. Others have presented false Social Security cards, which were never intended to be used as identification and are worthless in that respect.

The Secret Service urges everyone to carry unquestionable identification and show it when cashing a check, but it does not urge everyone to go to as much trouble as one man did to identify himself. This man had his name, address, and veterans' serial number engraved on his false teeth. Whenever he was asked for identification he simply took them out. He was never suspected of forging a check.

VI

THE FINANCIAL SCOREBOARD

THE Secretary of the Treasury and the Treasurer of the United States are often thought to be one and the same. In reality they are different persons occupying two very different offices.

The Secretary of the Treasury, of course, is the head of the entire Treasury Department, and he is a member of the President's Cabinet. All operations and functions of the department are his responsibility.

The Treasurer of the United States is the official custodian of the Government's funds. He or she—several women have held this high post—directs the Government's banking operations, just as the president of a private bank would do. He is charged with receiving and paying out the Treasury's money, keeping accounts of these transactions, and preparing daily and monthly statements which show how much has been spent, how much has been received, and the size of the Treasury's balance.

It is the Treasurer of the United States who issues Government checks—more than 350,000,000 a year. Money paid into the Treasury by any one of a dozen Government departments and bureaus, such as Customs and Internal Revenue, and by millions of employers in all parts of the country, is deposited first in 11,000 private banks. They report how much they receive, and twice a week an Assistant Secretary adds it all up so that the Treasury knows how much it has available at all times.

Although this money belongs to the Government, bankers are allowed to lend a certain part of it without paying interest. This privilege is accorded them in return for performing numerous services for the Treasury, such as selling and cashing savings bonds. When the Treasury needs any of its money that is in private banks, it issues a "call." The amount called for is then sent by the private banks to Federal Reserve banks, where it is put into the account of the Treasurer of the United States. Usually the Treasurer keeps a balance of between $450,000,000 and $500,000,000 in his account with the Federal Reserve banks.

There are about 2,000 disbursing offices, located in all parts of the country, which can issue Government checks. They draw them against the Treasurer's account in the Federal Reserve banks. The gigantic job of writing more than 350,000,000 checks each year would be impossible if it were not for automation. Machines do the work. Some of them turn out as many as 4,000 checks an hour, each check bearing a different name and address and stating that it is worth a certain amount to its owner. Automatic tabulators and recorders provide a permanent record of the amount of each check, to whom it was paid, and when it was issued.

Forged Government checks are returned first to the Treasurer, who makes a record of them and sends them on to the Secret Service, which promptly sets out to catch the forgers.

One of the most interesting and difficult duties performed by the office of the Treasurer of the United States has to do with mutilated or burned money sent in with the hope of receiving new money for it. The Treasurer employs experts to work on the hundreds of cases received every year, and their brilliant scientific detective work has saved people countless millions that would otherwise have been lost.

Even though it is printed on the finest paper that can be manufactured—an American dollar bill can take more than two thousand double foldings in the same crease without tearing—our paper money does wear out. The Treasurer is glad to replace old or worn-out bills with crisp new ones. Hundreds of millions of dollars worth of old bills are burned in the Treasurer's furnaces every year. Anyone can take a torn or worn-out bill to a bank and receive a new one for it, after which the bank sends it to the Treasurer to be destroyed.

Replacing burned or badly mutilated money, however, poses greater and more complicated problems. The Treasurer has a general rule that applies in most cases: If three-fifths of the damaged money can be identified, the full amount is repaid. If only two fifths of it can be identified, half its face value is repaid. When less than two fifths is identifiable, it falls into a special category and the case is assigned to an expert.

The identification of currency from mere fragments, some of which may be completely charred, is a job that only a trained money detective can perform. It requires a thorough knowledge of all United States paper currency, limitless patience, a delicate touch, the use of scientific aids such as chemicals, and of simple tools such as pins, tweezers, blotters, cotton, strong lights, and magnifying glasses—and last but not the least in importance, a determination to do a good job.

When the Nazis invaded Austria before World War II, one Austrian businessman was forced to abandon his company and flee with his father to Switzerland. They took with them $33,000 in American currency. The businessman went on alone to Argentina, leaving the money with his father. From South America he wrote his father to turn the money over to a friend who would send it to him by surreptitious means.

The friend tried to get the money out of the country but failed, and at last decided to hide it for the duration of the war. His choice of a hiding place was ingenious. Putting the bills into a small wooden cylinder, he cut a hole in a tree, inserted the cylinder, and carefully replaced the bark.

After the war, the Austrian businessman returned and he and his friend recovered the money from the tree. The cylinder was intact, but the bills in it had deteriorated to such an extent that they were unusable.

The money was sent to the Treasurer in Washington. After long and patient work, a money detective was able to identify most of it and the Austrian was repaid.

Recently a North Carolina farmer was called away unexpectedly, but before leaving, he hid $600 which he did not want to chance carrying with him. His choice of a hiding place produced a curious result. He placed the bills in a small glass jar and put the jar in the flue of the kitchen stove. The day he returned from his trip was cold, so he quickly built a fire in the stove. By the time he had remembered the hidden money, the bills were severely charred, but luckily for him, they were nicely preserved in molten glass, and an expert was able to identify them.

Not long ago a California man visited the graves of his parents on Memorial Day. As he was putting flowers on them his foot touched something that felt like metal. Digging into the ground, he extracted a small can, and in making a further search he found several others buried only a few inches beneath the surface. Inside each can was a soft substance which looked like deteriorated paper money.

Without disturbing the contents of the cans, the man sent them to the Treasurer. After painstaking work, an expert was able to identify $23,000 in American currency, and that amount was paid to the man. The man's father had buried

BLAIRSVILLE SENIOR HIGH SCHOOL
BLAIRSVILLE, PENNA.

the money in the cemetery plot several years before he was placed there himself.

One afternoon a Pennsylvania woman was spading a bed in her back yard. At first she thought her spade had struck part of a rotted stump or a root, but after prodding a bit further she unearthed the corner of a wooden crate. The spade had broken open a slat of the crate, and through the opening she could see what appeared to be soggy and moldy currency. She hurried to her bank for advice and was told to send the money to the Treasurer. In due time she received a check from the Treasurer for $9,714, as experts had been able to identify that much of the money. It was never learned who had buried the treasure in the woman's back yard.

One of the oddest stories about damaged currency involved a farmer and a cow. The farmer lost his wallet containing $600 while feeding his stock, and after searching in vain for it, he became convinced that one of the animals had eaten it. He selected a cow as the culprit, and luck was with him. After he had butchered the cow, he found the partially digested bills in its' stomach. The currency expert to whom it was sent was able to identify $473 of the $600 that had been in the wallet, and the Treasurer paid the farmer that amount.

Employees in the damaged money section of the Treasurer's office tell about the Minnesota farmer who buried a strongbox full of paper money in a wheat field. He disliked banks, and he thought his savings would be safe hidden in his own land. Several years later he needed the money, but when he dug up the strongbox he found that the bills had become fused into a hardened mass. He sent the box to the Treasurer with a claim that it had contained $20,000. The farmer was wrong. Experts identified $27,000 in the box.

Not so pleasant is the story of the elderly West Virginia man and his wife. It was rumored that they had a fortune buried on their farm. One day two thieves appeared and ransacked the house. When the old couple refused to reveal where the money was hidden, they were brutally murdered, and the thieves set fire to the home to cover their terrible crime. They were caught and executed. Some time later, while looking through the ruins, a son of the man and woman found beneath the kitchen floor several cans containing badly burned currency. He sent it to the Treasurer for redemption and received a check for $6,000, the entire amount the cans had contained.

Other sections of the national scoreboard record the work of the Bureau of Accounts, the Office of the Comptroller General of the Currency, and the Bureau of Public Debt—all departments of the Treasury. These may appear to be imposing titles, but the duties of each can be simply explained.

The Bureau of Accounts does exactly what its name indicates—it keeps the books of the Treasury Department. It is to the Bureau of Accounts that the Secretary of the Treasury goes if he wants to know the condition of the Government's finances, how much money all his departments took in last month, or how much each one of them spent last year. Such information is ready for him at all times.

But the Bureau of Accounts has numerous other duties in addition to bookkeeping. It prepares the reports which the Secretary of the Treasury must make periodically to the President, the Congress, the Bureau of the Budget, and the public. It handles the enormous investment accounts of the Government—the buying and selling of Treasury bonds. If a foreign government awards money to an American on a claim, the Bureau makes the payment. It administers the complicated problems involving the deposit of withheld taxes in banks. It processes claims made by Americans for valuables lost in shipment. It supervises matters having to do with fidelity and surety bonds.

The Comptroller General of the Currency has supervision over all national banks, including the organization of new banks and bank mergers, and he appoints receivers for any banks that fail. Four times a year every national bank must submit a report to him on its condition. At least three times every two years, agents of the Comptroller examine the books of all national banks in the United States to determine whether they are obeying Federal laws and whether they are solvent.

Two of the most common questions people ask when they visit or write the Treasury Department are: "What is the national debt?" and "What does it mean?"

In simple terms, the national debt—which is also called the public debt—is like a bank loan or any other kind of financial debt. In this case, the United States owes it to people who have lent the Government money.

When people buy Government securities, such as Treasury bonds and savings bonds, they are lending the Government their money. Interest is paid to them on these loans, just as a private bank pays you interest on the money in your savings account.

Inasmuch as transactions of these kinds have to do with how much money the Government owes, they quite properly are supervised by the Bureau of Public Debt. They are big business. Every working day of the year millions of dollars worth of Treasury securities are bought and sold. There are two groups of them, called marketable and non-marketable.

The first group is handled by security exchanges throughout the country (like stock exchanges), by investment houses, and by banks. Usually they are bought and sold in large amounts which are beyond the reach of small investors, although no one is prohibited from acquiring them.

When the Treasury wants to borrow money by selling a new bond issue, the Bureau of Public Debt prepares circulars explaining the new "offering." It issues instructions on when and how it may be sold, how much interest will be paid, and other pertinent details, and the Bureau handles subscriptions for it, regulates allotments to purchasers, and handles all other transactions connected with it.

The largest group of nonmarketable securities is savings bonds. They are called nonmarketable simply because they cannot be bought and sold in public markets, such as stock and bond exchanges. Only individuals may buy and sell them, either directly from the Treasury or from banks.

Keeping track of transactions in savings bonds is an almost insuperable task. Every time one is bought or sold, a record must be made. But the job has to be done, for the Treasury could not depend entirely on wealthy individuals and corporations to lend it money. If it did that, it could not get as much as it needs. Hundreds of billions of dollars are held by the public in millions of savings accounts throughout the nation. The Treasury must have a means of borrowing a part of this money.

That means is savings bonds. Any person with $18.75 can buy a $25 savings bond. The Bureau of Public Debt sees that the buyer of the bond is paid interest, until at the end of seven years nine months the buyer has received $25 for the $18.75 he or she lent the United States.

More than $48,000,000,000 worth of savings bonds are outstanding. That means savings bonds worth that much are in the possession of Americans. Under the law all of them could be cashed at one time. Of course, that would not happen, but it is one of the good things about savings bonds. Every person who owns one has the comforting feeling of knowing he can get his money in cash whenever he wants it.

Every day millions of people do want their money, and turn in their savings bonds. On the other hand, every day millions of other people buy bonds. It is this ceaseless buying and selling that inflicts on the Bureau of Public Debt its greatest accounting burden.

In the Bureau's offices are 2,500,000,000 records of transactions in savings bonds!

Savings bonds, like paper currency, can be lost, damaged or destroyed. That is one reason—indeed, the main one as far as the public is concerned—why the 2,500,000,000 records in the Bureau are of incalculable value.

The Bureau has issued more than a million substitute bonds. It is sincerely sympathetic to persons whose bonds have been lost or destroyed, and it makes every effort to replace them, just as the Treasurer does when paper money is damaged.

A brief look into our history helps us to understand much about the public debt. Since President Washington took the oath of office, in 1789, a lot of things have happened to the United States Government, and most of them have cost money.

In that period the Government has spent about $1,500,-000,000,000. It has taken in about $1,200,000,000,000. The difference of $300,000,000,000 is the national debt—what the Government owes.

When Alexander Hamilton became the first Secretary of the Treasury the public debt already existed. Hamilton found himself faced with bills for $78,000,000, a towering sum in those days. These, our first debts, were the unpaid cost of the Revolutionary War.

A number of people thought that the new and poor Government should not attempt to pay off the Revolutionary War debt at 100 cents on the dollar, but should force those to whom the money was due to take less in settlement. Perhaps no more courageous step ever was taken by a Secretary of the Treasury than by Hamilton when he pledged that the Government would pay off every penny it owed in full. Hamilton knew that would be the surest way to establish confidence in the integrity of the struggling new nation.

The policy of Hamilton, supported by the great moral force of George Washington, was adopted by a reluctant

Congress and carried out, but not without difficulty. Probably the most important result was that the foundation was laid for making the American dollar a standard of value throughout the whole world. "Sound as a dollar" took the place of "Not worth a Continental."

The Treasury today is faced with problems not unlike those which burdened Hamilton. The long duration of World War II and the cold war now going on have produced an inflation which has seriously reduced the buying power of the dollar and have brought hardship to many people, especially to those who are obliged to live on what are called "fixed incomes," such as pensions or the interest from savings.

Just as they did in Hamilton's time, some people today believe the public debt cannot be paid off in full. They say: "What's the use of saving your money? It buys less and less." Some economists have gone so far as to predict that the United States will face continually rising prices and a gradual decline in the value of money.

The Treasury Department does not believe these things. Quite to the contrary, it believes that the United States can have sound, stable money which will retain its value down through the years.

Yes, says the Treasury, the public debt is large. It is too big to be paid off all at once. But good management, the Treasury declares, can keep the burden of the public debt from hampering the country's growth.

More than $210,000,000,000 of the $300,000,000,000 public debt came from World War II. While the Government's income increased eightfold during the war, it was still necessary to borrow huge sums to achieve victory.

Since 1946 the public debt has increased about $30,000,-000,000. This is largely because the cold war has forced us to continue heavy expenditures for national defense. A much smaller part has been the result of mild recessions, during which the Government's income fell while at the same time it was obliged to launch programs that would decrease unemployment and increase spending for the national defense.

Since 1946 our population has grown faster than the public debt. There has been a 28 per cent increase in population and a 12 per cent debt increase. Dividing the debt by our population gives us what is called our per capita debt. In 1946 it was $1,832 for every American, and at present it is about $1,600.

If we consider the debt in terms of what we produce in this country, the debt burden has been reduced by 50 per cent. In 1946 the debt amounted to 116 per cent of our gross national product,* and in 1962 it amounted to about 58 per cent.

One step which the Treasury advocates for reducing the debt is the inclusion in the annual Federal budget of a certain amount of money—perhaps a billion dollars—for that specific purpose. In this way some payment on the debt would be assured every year.

However, this would not be sufficient to guarantee a steady reduction of the debt unless the Government's income were enough to pay for its expenses. If it weren't enough, the Treasury would have to borrow more money to meet its obligations.

It is utterly impossible for the Government to predict accurately how much money it will need in the year ahead. For one thing, the cold war being carried on by Communist nations prevents such an estimate. Expenses for defense might have to be increased overnight.

* Gross national product means the total of all goods and services produced in the United States, from shoelaces to missiles, from medical treatments to dry cleaning—everything. In recent times the gross national product has amounted to well over $500,000,000,000.

The Treasury says frankly and plainly that the only sure way to reduce the debt is for the Government to spend less than it takes in. The Government, declares the Treasury, should strive to end a year with surplus money in its safe, and this unneeded money should be used to reduce the public debt.

VII

HAMILTON'S NAVY

BEFORE the American Revolution smugglers were patriots and patriots were smugglers. The Thirteen Colonies were struggling to defeat the policy of "taxation without representation," which had been imposed on them by the Government of England. Respectable citizens like John Hancock and Samuel Adams, both signers of the Declaration of Independence, were smugglers. In those times it was considered a patriotic act to smuggle goods into the Colonies, and out of them, without paying taxes to the British.

By the time the Revolution was over and the United States of America had been born, smuggling had become a habit of the American people. The government of the new republic, however, took a different view of the matter. It needed money desperately, and smuggling deprived it of taxes and revenues to which it was entitled. Instead of being looked upon as a patriotic activity, smuggling was seen in its true guise—a violation of the law.

As the first Secretary of the Treasury, Alexander Hamilton had the difficult task of stopping it. He tackled the job with his customary energy and forthrightness. In 1790, only a year after Washington had been sworn in as the first president, Hamilton asked Congress for "ten boats" to guard the coast against smugglers. The request was granted, Washington signed the legislation, and the Coast Guard was created.

It was easy for Hamilton to convince citizens that duties collected on imports and exports were "taxation *with* representation." The money taken in went toward paying the expenses of the Government, and thereby made other forms of taxation unnecessary. But it was not as easy to convince the people that smuggling was a crime and that smugglers were criminals. For some time the apathy of many Americans was a major antagonist in Hamilton's war against violators of the new customs laws.

Hamilton's "ten boats" were cutter types—that is, heavy-keeled schooners that could carry a large amount of sail to give them speed. They ranged from 36 to 40 feet in length and were armed with swivel guns. The cost was about $1,000 each.

The first to be constructed was the two-masted *Massachusetts*, launched at Newburyport, Massachusetts, in 1791. She displaced about 70 tons. Her six swivel guns made her the most formidable cutter in the fleet. After the *Massachusetts* came the 51-ton *Scammel*, the *Active* and the *Pickering*, 50 tons each, the 40-ton *Diligence*, and the *Argus*, the *Vigilant*, the *Virginia*, and the *South Carolina*, each of 35 tons and carrying four guns. The *General Greene*, a 30-ton sloop, was armed with only three.

Hamilton engaged men of "respectable character" to sail his fleet. Captains received $30 a month, first mates $20, second mates $16, third mates $14, sailors $8, and cabin boys $4.

The first captain sworn in was Hopley Yeaton of New Hampshire, who had served as a third officer in the Continental Navy. Two other cutter captains, John Foster Williams and David Porter, were former sea fighters. The others were civilian seamen. All wore cocked hats over hair tied up in short queues, blue swallow-tailed coats with gold buttons and epaulets, knee breeches, and boots. On deck they wore side arms and carried speaking trumpets through which they shouted their commands. The sailors of Hamilton's little fleet also wore their hair in pigtails, which they tarred for protection against salt water. The broad sailor's collar was designed to catch drippings from the waterproofed queues. When they dressed up to go ashore, the sailors sported hard black hats with flat brims and pillbox crowns, short blue jackets with brass buttons, and bell-bottomed trousers.

This was the small beginning of the great United States Coast Guard we know today. Early in its history it distinguished itself, and it has never ceased to be feared, respected, and honored. Hamilton's fighting sailors and their cutters became the scourge of smugglers from Georgia to Canada. So effective was their work that they soon received increases in pay and subsistence.

The Coast Guard began as an adjunct of the Treasury Department, and it has been that ever since, but through the years its duties and assignments have steadily increased. Now it is a full arm of America's fighting forces, on land, on the sea, and in the air.

During World War II, when Coast Guard operations were co-ordinated with those of the Navy, it had 802 ships over 65 feet in length and it manned 351 Navy and 288 Army craft. Its shore installations numbered 1,096. Its manpower reached a peak of 171,168, and of these men more than half served on ships. It was then that women were enlisted for the first time in the Coast Guard. More than 10,000 of them donned the smart uniform of the SPARS and made it possible for more men to be sent to fighting fronts.

For the first eight years Hamilton's cutters were the young nation's only navy. The regular American Navy was not organized until 1798. During this period, a diplomatic war of nerves France was waging against the United States had broken out into an undeclared shooting war at sea. French privateers had captured more than 340 American ships. The

Coast Guard cutters joined the young Navy in the war against the French raiders, and with this act became part of American fighting forces. One of the early cutters, the *Eagle*, covered itself with glory, capturing 5 French ships itself and assisting in the capture of 10 others. The *Eagle* also recovered 7 captured American ships. Her sister cutter, the *Pickering*, fought a notable engagement with the privateer, *L'Égypte Conquise*. The French ship had double the firepower of the *Pickering* and a crew three times as large, but at the end of nine hours she had become so battered that she hauled down the tricolor and surrendered.

Nine Coast Guard cutters, averaging 125 tons each, fought in the War of 1812. The conflict was not a week old when the cutter *Jefferson* captured the British ship *Patriot*, the first prize to fall into American hands. Altogether the cutters took 14 enemy ships.

England was a great sea power and was able to send strong squadrons into American waters. Frequently the cutters found themselves up against bigger, more heavily armed warships. Cutters went down to defeat on several occasions, but not before they had fought to the very end of their strength. In June, 1813, three British boats slipped up on the 75-ton cutter *Surveyor*, at night in the York River, Virginia. Though outnumbered 50 to 15, the cutter crew wounded 7 and killed 3 of the enemy before being overwhelmed. British Captain John Crerie was so impressed by "the determined way in which her deck was disputed, inch by inch," in hand-to-hand fighting, that he returned to William Travis, captain of the cutter, "the sword you so nobly used."

Another notable battle in the War of 1812 ensued when the cutter *Eagle*, carrying six guns, met the British war vessel, *Dispatch*, which mounted eighteen guns, off Long Island. After the cutter had been badly damaged, its crew ran her aground and then dragged her four-pounders to the top of a bluff. Salvaging the small shot that had riddled the *Eagle*'s hull, they made cartridges from bits of cloth and pages from the cutter's log and they fired the shot back at the British. So telling was this fire that the British ship was forced to withdraw.

The Coast Guard has never forgotten the *Eagle*. Today cadets are trained on a modern *Eagle*.

No sooner had the War of 1812 ended than the cutters were ordered to war against pirates and slave ships, and a number of privateers were run down and captured in the waters off the south Atlantic coast. The importation of slaves was forbidden by Federal law, and the job of halting the inhumane traffic was another duty handed to the Coast Guard. Slavers were halted and the Coast Guard freed more than 500 Negroes, who were being brought from Africa to the southern states.

However, not only wars against smugglers, enemy invaders, and slavers occupied the time of the Coast Guard in its early years, but it was also called upon to fight Indians and to settle domestic troubles, too.

In 1832 there was trouble in the wind when South Carolina decided to remove duties on imports entering through her ports. Five cutters were promptly dispatched to Charleston to enforce the collection of customs, and President Andrew Jackson declared: "If a single drop of blood shall be shed in opposition to the laws of the United States, I will hang the first man I can lay my hands on upon the first tree I can reach." South Carolina quickly got back into line and obeyed the law.

In 1836, the Seminole Indians were on the warpath in Florida, and eight cutters were ordered to the scene. The cutter *Washington* arrived just in time to land men and guns to save Fort Brook, after the Seminoles had ambushed the soldiers defending the post and massacred all but one. This was the first amphibious landing by combined forces in United States history, and it anticipated by more than one hundred years the great landings carried out by the Coast Guard in World War II.

The cutters continued to co-operate with the Army and Navy in Florida for nearly three years, blockading rivers, carrying dispatches, transporting troops and ammunition, and providing landing parties for the defense of settlements. When the war with the Seminoles finally ended, each Coast Guardsman who had served in it was rewarded with a grant of 160 acres of land in Florida.

The first iron ships of the Coast Guard were built just in time to participate in actions of the war with Mexico. The steam cutters *Forward* and *McLane* aided in an amphibious operation at the mouth of the Tabasco River.

Like the men of the Army and Navy, Coast Guardsmen fought on both sides during the Civil War. Five cutters were seized in southern waters by Confederate forces. Oddly enough, the cutter *Harriet Lane* fought at different times under the Stars and Stripes and under the Stars and Bars.

The *Harriet Lane* fired the first shot of the war in April, 1861, on the eve of the bombardment of Fort Sumter. Coming upon a southern ship trying to run into Charleston harbor without showing a flag, she put a shot across its bow and halted it. Later the *Harriet Lane* participated in the first Union victory, the capture of Fort Clark and Fort Hatteras, which were bases for blockade runners in Hatteras Inlet. Then, transferred to the Navy, she served as the flagship of Adm. David Porter, whose grandfather had been a captain of one of Hamilton's original ten cutters. At Galveston she was captured, and she finished the war as a Confederate ship.

The cutter *Naugatuck* escorted the *Monitor* when she sailed out of Hampton Roads in March, 1862, to do battle with the Confederate ironclad *Merrimac*. The cutter *Miami* saw action at Willoughby's Point, where she landed President Lincoln on Confederate-held soil the day before the fall of Norfolk.

After the Civil War the cutters returned to patrolling the coastal lanes, guarding shipping and fighting smugglers, and until the Spanish-American War they enjoyed a relatively long period of peace. The outbreak of the Spanish-American War found the cutter *McCulloch* en route to San Francisco via the Mediterranean and the Suez Canal. At Singapore she was ordered to join Admiral Dewey's forces in the Philippines. She distinguished herself in the Battle of Manila Bay, after which she raced to Hong Kong with news of the American victory so it could be cabled to the world. Altogether there were 18 cutters in the war with Spain, 8 of them in action in Cuban waters.

"Plan 1, Acknowledge."

That was the dispatch received by all Coast Guard units on the morning of April 6, 1917. It meant that the United States was at war with Germany, and that the Coast Guard was to go into action with the Navy immediately.

Thereafter in rapid succession came vicious battles between Coast Guard cutters and German submarines in all parts of the Atlantic. Several cutters acquitted themselves with rare distinction. Perhaps the record of the *Seneca* best illustrates the intrepidity shown by Coast Guard ships in this great conflict.

On April 28, 1918, the *Seneca* was escorting Allied ships toward Gibraltar when a pack of three U-boats was encountered. The British naval sloop *Cowslip* was broken nearly in two by a torpedo. Under the circumstances, the *Seneca* would have been justified in steaming on, looking to the safety of the other ships and herself. But she stopped three times to put off lifeboats and pick up 81 survivors.

In another of the *Seneca*'s convoys the British collier *Wellington* was torpedoed. She was abandoned but remained afloat. Her crew refused to return to her. Men from the *Seneca*, 20 of them, boarded the crippled collier, got up steam, and started her for Brest. Then the British captain and

19 members of the *Wellington*'s crew returned to the collier. "I can't see others doing duty that is mine," the *Wellington*'s captain said.

During the night a gale came up, and the battered *Wellington* went down. The British destroyer *Warrington* picked up 7 survivors—6 British seamen and one American Coast Guardsman—in a lifeboat and 7 more seamen and 8 Coast Guardsmen were rescued from makeshift rafts. Thus 11 Coast Guardsmen had lost their lives.

The chief of the British Admiralty at the time was Winston Churchill. From the Admiralty came this message: "Seldom in the annals of the sea has there been exhibited such self-abnegation, such cool courage, and such unfailing diligence in the face of almost insurmountable difficulties."

The Coast Guard suffered greater losses, in proportion to its strength, than any of the other United States armed forces in World War 1.

Between the two great world wars the Coast Guard continued to grow. One of its most arduous duties was capturing rumrunners. This work was unpopular, unpleasant and dangerous, and the Coast Guardsmen were just as glad as were most Americans when the prohibition era ended.

When war in Europe broke out again in September, 1939, the Coast Guard, now three times larger than it had been during World War I, was ordered to carry out extensive patrols to insure that merchant ships in our waters did not violate the neutrality proclaimed by President Franklin D. Roosevelt. In one month, March of 1941, it took 28 Italian, 2 German, and 35 Danish ships into protective custody and interned their crews to prevent scuttling and sabotage.

After the disaster at Pearl Harbor, the cutters went into full-scale action against German U-boats. In the Atlantic alone the cutters destroyed 11 Nazi submarines and rescued more than 4,000 survivors of torpedoings. The cutter *Icarus* blasted a U-boat to the surface and captured its crew.

Seven cutters were lost in fierce sea battles with sub packs. Coast Guardsmen manned landing crafts that hit the beaches at Guadalcanal, North Africa, Normandy, Iwo Jima, and a score of other places, not infrequently with unforgettable service "beyond the call of duty." On D day in Normandy Coast Guard cutters were given special lifesaving assignments. Under fire from German shore guns, they saved 1,468 survivors of sunken Army and Navy barges.

The cutter *Northland* captured the sealer *Buskoe* and frustrated a Nazi attempt to set up a weather station on Greenland. This was the first naval capture of the war. And while the cutters fought at sea and in the landings, other Coast Guard contingents patrolled every foot of the 40,000 miles of American shore line. It was a Coast Guardsman, John Cullen, who detected 4 Nazi saboteurs landing on Long Island from a German submarine. Their capture led to the apprehension by Federal Bureau of Investigation agents of 4 other Nazis who had made a similar landing in Florida.

Peace came, but the Coast Guard knew no rest. On the contrary, its duties were increased, its fields of operation were expanded. It became not only a fighting force, not only the guardian of our shores and the protector of shipping, but a scientific force holding a place of prominence in the scheme of modern America.

Today the Coast Guard carries on important work on many fronts.

Cutters, sleek and powerful ships more than 300 feet in length and carrying heavy armament, range the oceans of the world to protect American interests, and 20 different types of aircraft perform the same functions in the skies.

Icebreakers keep sea lanes open. Small, fast cutters patrol coastal waters, on guard night and day against the smugglers that still try occasionally to sneak contraband into the country without paying duty on it. Lightships ride at anchor in the entrances to important harbors, and far out at sea, in strategic places, meteorological readings are taken to aid in studying and forecasting the world's weather.

Between the months of February and August the Coast Guard maintains an ice patrol over an area of 45,000 square miles, about the size of Pennsylvania, in the North Atlantic. It is during this period of the year that great icebergs drift southward toward the busiest steamer lanes in the world.

The area patrolled is blanketed a large part of the time with heavy fogs. An average of 400 bergs are carried southward each year. Gradually they melt and vanish, but until that happens they are a serious menace to ships. A collision with a berg, three quarters of which is under water, means disaster.

The Coast Guard ice patrol destroys bergs when possible, but the size of some makes destruction difficult. Even if the top is blasted away, an enormous section may be left, and it will be as much of a menace as the entire berg. No chances are taken that this might happen. The precise location of every berg is charted, the direction of its course and the speed of its drift are determined, and this information is radioed to ships and shore stations.

The Coast Guard began its famed ice patrol in 1913, the year after the great British liner *Titanic*, making her maiden voyage to the United States, struck a berg and sank with a loss of more than 1,500 lives. After half a century the Coast Guard can proudly state that no ship has been lost in the area it patrols through collision with an iceberg.

It was in 1850 that Congress appropriated $10,000 to build lifeboat stations along the eastern coast and to provide "surfboats, rockets, carronades, and other apparatus for the better preservation of life and property from shipwrecks."

For more than five years these early lifesaving stations were manned by volunteers, called together like a volunteer fire department whenever there was a shipwreck. In 1854 station keepers were appointed at a salary of $200 a year.

It was not until 1871 that the Secretary of the Treasury was permitted to employ surfmen for the stations.

Between 1871 and World War II, Coast Guard cutters and lifeboat stations rescued 203,609 persons and saved nearly $2,000,000,000 worth of property in shipwrecks and floods. To accomplish this magnificent job, the Coast Guardsmen had to put to sea in the worst possible weather. One old surfman described his work this way: "All I know is the regulations book says you have to go out. It doesn't say anything about coming back."

But most of the surfmen who went out have come back. One of the reasons for their success is that years of experience in launching small boats through dangerous surf has developed a special, rugged breed of men. Another reason is that their equipment has been specially developed through years of trial and error.

Lifeboats provide good examples of how great improvements have been. There is the 26-foot surfboat that weighs nearly a ton and is propelled by oars. The same boat comes in a power model, and both types are self-bailing. Then there are two models of motor lifeboats, a 36-footer and a 52-footer. They are self-bailing, self-righting, virtually unsinkable, and they have enclosed, heated compartments.

The most fabulous of all lifesaving craft today, however, is the versatile amphibious truck, or DUKW. These vehicles can travel at 55 miles an hour on paved roads. Then, without stopping, they can partially deflate their tires for better traction on sand and move at 13 miles an hour across beaches. Continuing on into the water, also without a stop, they have a speed of 6 miles an hour. When they return from the water, they reinflate their tires and speed away.

The giant Marlin flying boats of the Coast Guard can travel 1,500 miles from shore, and they can land on the ocean to pick up survivors from a disaster or to pick up from a ship a person who needs medical attention. For shorter trips over water, and for rescuing persons in inaccessible areas, the Coast Guard has giant helicopters.

The Coast Guard enjoys the boast that it has had a hand in aviation from the very beginning. When the Wright brothers made their historic flight at Kitty Hawk, North Carolina, in 1903, three surfmen of the nearby Kill Devil Lifeboat Station were present. One of them took a picture of the plane as it flew a few feet above the sand. When, after the flight which electrified the world, wind flipped the plane over and threatened to wreck it, the three surfmen grabbed it and helped to tie it down safely.

When ships get into trouble at sea, the Coast Guard goes out and brings them in. But it does the same things for ships that are not in trouble, guiding them past rocks and shoals, through darkness and fog, with its 39,000 navigation aids—lighthouses, lightships, buoys, fog signals, and radio beacons. More than 500 fully manned lighthouses are under its jurisdiction. The tallest light in service is the 191-foot tower at Cape Charles, Virginia, but the highest light, although it has only a 43-foot tower, stands on Cape Mendocino, California, 422 feet above the Pacific. It can be seen 28 miles away.

The operation of coastal lights is a lot easier now than it was a few years ago, when smoky oil lamps had to be cleaned and filled and their wicks kept trimmed. Some of the lights and fog signals now in use are turned on and off by a remote radio control system called ANRAC. And there are other electronic wonders: RACON, which gives distance (up to 120 miles) and bearing of ships and planes from the beacons, and LORAN, which provides navigational information to air and surface craft. Coast Guard LORAN stations in Greenland, Newfoundland, Alaska, the Philippines, the Caribbean, and remote Pacific Islands, as well as in the continental United States, form a safety network over the north Atlantic and north Pacific oceans.

The first American ship to reach Alaska after the territory

was purchased from Russia in 1867 was the Coast Guard cutter *Lincoln.* In the years that followed, cutters dispatched on Alaskan duty were the chief symbol of the American Government in that remote land. More than that, they were guardian angels, good friends, and mother hens. For the Department of Justice they enforced the law, apprehended criminals, and served as floating courts. For the Navy they gathered military intelligence. For the Post Office Department they carried the mail. For the Interior Department they carried schoolteachers to their posts, checked on sanitation in ports, and protected timber and game. For the Department of Commerce they made surveys of the coast and surveys of industries. They transported Public Health Service doctors and nurses to isolated villages. The commanding officers of the cutters performed marriages.

Today, although Alaska is a full-fledged state of the Union, the Coast Guard still performs many of these same tasks in the Far North.

Its Alaska service symbolizes the Coast Guard: Wherever there are Americans to be protected and helped, the Coast Guard is on hand to do the job.

VIII

NARCOTICS AND MOONSHINE

THE names of the three brothers were Mohammed Oz Yurik, Ahmet Oz Yurik, and Halil Oz Yurik. They lived in a remote mountain region of Turkey. For several months two undercover agents of the Treasury's Bureau of Narcotics and officers of the Turkish police had been secretly observing their activities.

The three brothers were the leaders of a gang of manufacturers and peddlers of narcotics—morphine, opium, and other drugs which are popularly called "dope." They were desperate, heavily armed criminals. After weeks of patient work, one of the American agents had established himself in the Turkish underworld as a narcotics buyer. At last he was able to meet Mohammed Oz Yurik. This is known as a "contact." Mohammed Oz Yurik sold the undercover agent 31 kilograms, about 14 pounds, of morphine base. The long-hoped-for "buy" had been accomplished, and the agent had the evidence he needed to bring about the arrest of the gang.

Capturing the brothers and their henchmen, however, was another matter. The American agents wanted the entire gang, not just some members of it. To accomplish this feat meant going into the mountains. Because of the desperate character of the brothers and the difficulty of capturing them by surprise, the Turkish police tried to discourage the agents from making the attempt. But the agents would not be stopped.

Supported by several Turkish constables, they attacked the hideout of the dope peddlers, and took not only the three brothers into custody, but five gang members. In the house of Mohammed Oz Yurik, they seized 44 kilograms of morphine base powder, 680 kilograms of opium, and a large quantity of other ingredients used in narcotics. In the basement of the house they found a laboratory in which opium was converted into morphine. It was the largest laboratory ever captured in Turkey.

Another ring of narcotics dealers had been smashed by agents of the Bureau of Narcotics who had risked their lives in accomplishing the task. In the Bureau's files it was listed as a routine case. Facing death is almost a commonplace event in the careers of the unaccountably brave men who fight to halt the illicit dope traffic of the world.

In the same year that Mohammed Oz Yurik and his gang were arrested and imprisoned, Bureau of Narcotics agents smashed and captured three other groups of narcotics peddlers in Turkey. Each investigation was highly dangerous and demanded great personal risk.

Laws regulating the sale and manufacture of narcotics have been in Federal statute books since 1890, but it was not until 1930 that the Bureau of Narcotics was organized, and the brilliant and competent investigator, Harry J. Anslinger, was appointed its chief.

Under Anslinger's direction the Bureau quickly became the nemesis of dope peddlers. Long before he retired, after many years of service, the Bureau of Narcotics had been more successful and was more feared throughout the underworld of every country than any other organization of its kind. Although the Bureau is a permanent department of the Treasury, it has complete freedom to carry on its work, the greater part of which must be conducted in secrecy. All that is known to the public is that it employs an average of 250 agents, but the identity and whereabouts of most of these agents is as secret as the manner in which they carry out their perilous assignments. Criminals have killed 9 agents while in the performance of their duties.

The success of the Bureau is revealed through the court trials of the narcotics dealers they have captured. This alone is a record of which any police force in the world might well be proud. While the Secret Service special agents rely on shadowing, and the agents of the Treasury's Bureau of Intelligence build cases of tax evasion from records, the Narcotics Bureau agents combine these techniques with undercover work in ferreting out gangsters and drug peddlers, and bringing them before the courts. In doing this they are constantly exposed to a type of vicious criminal who does not hesitate to shoot or kill if the slightest mistake reveals the agent's identity.

During one recent year, agents of the Bureau of Narcotics captured and brought to justice 2,414 men and women who had violated drug laws. Enormous quantities of heroin, opium, marijuana, and cocain were seized and destroyed. These drugs were valued at millions of dollars.

The investigations made each year by the Bureau undercover agents would fill a dozen long novels of suspense, intrigue and violent crime. Not all of these secret operations are disclosed, of course, even when successfully completed, but those which are made public give an indication of the extent of the Bureau's work.

In one period of three months, Bureau agents, working with local authorities, captured three important gangs of narcotics dealers in Lebanon. Other investigations were carried out with success in Iran, Italy, Canada, Mexico, and several other foreign countries.

The war carried on by the Bureau against the evil and illicit traffic in drugs never ceases, and there can be no peace, for as swiftly as gangs and individual sellers are eliminated, others appear to take their places. The enormous profits to be made prove irresistible to criminals. The fact that most drug peddlers and their accomplices reach the end of their trails behind the bars of Federal prisons does not seem to prevent men and women from attempting to outwit the agents of the Bureau of Narcotics.

In one recent case this attitude was shown to exist in the seven brothers of the Campisi family of Newark, New Jersey. They worked their way up in the illegal drug trade until they had become associated with top gangsters of the powerful Mafia, including Salvatore Lucania, better known to the world as Lucky Luciano. The Campisis largely controlled the heroin traffic in New York, and they were a major source for this drug for most of the United States. They had smuggled immense quantities of it into the country, aided by their underworld associates in Italy and Sicily.

Around the Campisis was a formidable wall of protection, but the Bureau agents worked patiently to break through it. At last they were successful. Charles Campisi made the mistake of selling 9 ounces of heroin to a Bureau undercover agent who posed as a peddler. Another agent discovered that the son of one of the brothers, Thomas Campisi, was a narcotics addict. The trail of the son led to a "contact" with Thomas, and a purchase was made. With two doors open, agents invaded the Campisi underworld empire and destroyed it.

Agents may spend weeks, even months, tracking down and apprehending a narcotics peddler. This happened in a recent New York City case. The Bureau heard from one of its stool pigeons that a man named Nathan Behrman had a large quantity of drugs for sale. They shadowed Behrman twenty-four hours a day for several weeks before he led them to his hideout where the illicit drugs were cached. In arresting him they also captured his chief associate, Anthony J.

Velluci, and more than 13 kilograms of almost pure heroin. It was one of the largest seizures ever made.

After a lengthy period of observation, agents arrested two women drug peddlers in Chicago, Clotele Saddler and Annie Clay, with 40 ounces of heroin. Clotele Saddler's husband Joseph got away from them, but he was trailed and eventually captured in the South, where he was peddling drugs on a large scale.

For several years the Bureau agents had known of a narcotics dealer called "*El Chocolate*." His headquarters were in San Antonio, Texas, but all efforts to learn his real name and locate him had failed. Inhabitants of the San Antonio underworld either knew little about him or were afraid to disclose any information as to his true identity. At last an agent living in the underworld as a criminal learned that El Chocolate's name was Edward Perez Barrientes. He was soon traced to his home and arrested with 9 ounces of heroin in his possession.

Similar undercover watchfulness by agents resulted in the arrest, in Oakland, California, of Wong Chong Wing and Gee Gim Tuck, and in the confiscation of several pounds of smoking opium.

No two cases are alike in detail, yet all cases have similar aspects, whether they be in Houston, Los Angeles, Detroit, Cleveland, Pittsburgh, Atlanta, or some other city. Unlike any other type of crime, the illegal traffic in drugs is complicated by inescapable operations, and it is these operations that keep the prices of narcotics high. A drug first must be smuggled into the United States. This means that the smugglers must be paid before they pass it on to the dealers. The dealers take their profit before they turn it over to runners for delivery to peddlers. The runners must be paid. In turn, the peddler must get his profit before he sells it to the unfortunate addicts. The operations of a bank robber, jewel thief, or burglar are simple by comparison.

Peddlers and addicts, the most exposed links in this evil chain, are often easily trailed, but the smugglers and dealers live in the half-light of a well-guarded underworld, and reaching them is extremely difficult. They are the prizes which the agents want the most. When a top man is captured, a chain is broken.

Almost all major drugs originate outside the United States, and that is the reason—to stop them at their source—that the Bureau of Narcotics carries its war across the seas.

In this important phase of their operations, the narcotics agents are greatly assisted by the Bureau of Customs. In numerous instances information picked up abroad by undercover agents is relayed to Customs inspectors, and by this means another strong barrier is built before the narcotics smuggler.

Quite often, however, Customs inspectors uncover smuggled narcotics without any forewarning. An important seizure of European heroin was made recently in New York when an alert Customs inspector discovered 56 ounces in a special vest worn by Giuseppe Indelicato, who was on his honeymoon from Italy. His bride spent a lonely five years while Indelicato served a sentence in prison.

The largest marijuana case in Customs records arose at Laredo, Texas, when José Ramon Mills Ortiz, a Puerto Rican resident of Chicago, was found by a Customs inspector to have 141 pounds of the drug concealed under the hood of his automobile. Ortiz attacked the inspector and attempted to escape, but was subdued and taken to jail.

Shortly thereafter, another Laredo inspector held a Puerto Rican woman who was entering the United States in a taxi. He had spotted a number written on the inside of her purse which was the same as the license number on Ortiz's car. The Customs men had in their possession a photograph taken from Ortiz, which proved to be a picture of the woman's husband, a man named Chavez. This circumstance led the inspectors to the discovery that Ortiz, Chavez, and his wife had gone to Mexico together from Chicago in two cars. Chavez was still in Mexico, and the Customs men began a search for him and the second car.

The next day an inspector happened to glance out the window of his apartment in Laredo. His trained eyes fell at once on a car that was like the one for which a search was being made. He investigated. Under the hood were sixty pounds of marijuana. The ownership of the car was traced to Chavez, but he obviously had abandoned it and disappeared.

Bureau of Narcotics agents, Customs inspectors, and Texas rangers recently worked together on a case in McAllen, Texas, which ended with the capture of Daniel Cantu Cantu; his brother, Jesus Cantu Cantu; and several of their co-conspirators; and the seizure of 188 pounds of marijuana which they had just smuggled in from Mexico. The arrest of these narcotics dealers required both great courage and skill. Daniel Cantu Cantu, a convicted murderer, had threatened to kill the first officer he met, and the others were notoriously dangerous criminals.

Although prohibition ended years ago in the United States, the making of illegal whisky and alcohol has continued on a large scale. Like peddlers of narcotics, captured moonshiners have their places taken quickly by others. Moreover, moonshiners outnumber dope peddlers many times, and more than 1,000 Treasury Department agents are kept busy pursuing them.

The office out of which these agents work bears what is probably the longest title of any bureau in the Treasury Department. It is known as the Enforcement Branch of the Alcohol and Tobacco Tax Division of the Internal Revenue Service. Although the main task of the agents is to apprehend persons who make and sell whisky and alcohol without paying a Federal tax on them, they do have other duties. Among them is stopping the illegal manufacture and sale of firearms and ammunition and preventing such lethal weapons as machine guns from reaching the hands of criminals.

Since the founding of the United States, the Government has levied a heavy tax on distilled spirits (now about $10.50 a gallon), and since the signing of the Constitution, escaping from the payment of that tax has been one of the most popular illegal occupations. In the early years of the nation not all moonshiners were criminals. Many people who were otherwise respectable distilled their own liquors in secret. They considered the taxing of it an invasion of their freedom and of their private rights. Respectable moonshiners no longer exist, however. Bootlegging is now carried on altogether by persons without character and with no respect for our laws. In some cases it is big business, and is controlled by gangsters and master criminals. But the little one-man still continues to operate in many rural areas, especially in the backwoods areas of the South, greatly to the aggravation of the agents of the Alcohol Tax Unit, for no sooner is one destroyed than another is built in some remote hill hollow. Eradicating them is a never-ending task.

The work of capturing bootleggers is as dangerous as it is continuous. Since the repeal of prohibition in 1933, an average of more than one agent a year has died under the fire of moonshiners' guns. Today's moonshiners are not only armed, but they are aided by modern equipment, such as telephones, radios, and fast cars that can emit dense clouds of black oil smoke to help them in escaping from pursuing agents.

The manpower of the Alcohol Tax Unit has been increased several times in the last decade. There are more agents in the field now than ever before, their efficiency steadily improves, and the number of bootleggers and illicit stills they capture steadily mounts, yet moonshining continues to increase.

To gather some idea of the situation, consider a recent report made by the Commissioner of Internal Revenue:

In a single year, agents of the Alcohol Tax Unit destroyed

14,498 illicit stills, an increase of more than 15 per cent over the previous year; confiscated more than 250,000 gallons of illegal liquor, an increase of 20 per cent; destroyed 8,641,586 gallons of mash from which whisky was to be made, a rise of more than 17 per cent; arrested 11,380 bootleggers, 8 per cent more than in the previous year; seized property valued at $3,851,185, including 3,242 automobiles, a gain of 18 per cent.

Not all of these increases were the result of greater bootlegging activity, but most of them were. Some of the gains in captures and confiscations came as a result of having an increased number of well-trained agents in the field.

The vast majority of these cases occurred in fourteen southern states, traditional centers of moonshine production. More than 96 per cent of the stills captured and 86 per cent of the arrests made were in the South.

One of the most interesting cases involved 11 persons in Lexington County, South Carolina. These enterprising moonshiners, most of whom had long records in that illegal business, installed smoke-screen devices on their automobiles in the hope of foiling pursuit by the Federal agents. When they were captured in the act of delivering moonshine to customers, they learned to their sorrow that distilling whisky illegally would not be the only charge against them. A law had been passed making the use of any smoke device on an automobile a serious Federal offense. Under it a violator could be fined $5,000 and sent to prison for ten years. That was the sentence each received.

Not long ago, in a period of three months, revenue agents —or "revenooers," as they are called by hillbillies—captured a score of illegal stills in Haralson, Carrol, Meriweather, and Upson Counties in Georgia, and in Cleburne County in Alabama, and arrested and convicted 24 moonshiners. The operators of these stills had evaded payment of more than $500,000 in Federal taxes on the whisky produced and sold before the agents caught up with them.

But not all important moonshine violations occur in the South. Recently 5 men were sentenced to serve ten years in prison for operating an illicit still on a New Jersey farm.

The hard-pressed agents of the Alcohol Tax Unit are beginning to use a weapon which may bring them greater success in capturing moonshiners, especially those distilling illegal corn whisky in isolated hill sections of the southern states. It will be much more difficult for them to hide their stills from helicopters hovering over the treetops, ready to swoop down and discharge armed agents any place and at any moment. And smoke throwers on cars will be of no help in escaping from agents pursuing in the air.

IX

TAXES, CHEATERS, AND SLEUTHS

A BRANCH office of the Internal Revenue Service received $20 worth of quarters with an income tax return. The quarters were sent by a woman who said she had been told to pay her taxes "quarterly."

Not everyone can be expected to understand the income tax laws, but anyone can understand why we must have taxes. Without them a government could not exist. Without them there could be no Army, Navy, or Air Force; there could be no enforcement of the laws, no Public Health Service, and without these protections we could not develop or progress—in fact, we could not survive as a nation.

The Internal Revenue Service, which collects taxes, is the largest department of the Treasury. Of the more than 50,000 Treasury employees, 5 out of 8 work in the Washington headquarters, the 9 regional offices, or the 61 district offices.

About 90 per cent of the Government's income is harvested each year by the Internal Revenue Service. During the last year the Service received 94,000,000 tax returns, and it poured into the Treasury's vault more than $92,000,000,000.

These figures explain the Service's importance and its huge size.

The basic individual income tax law we know today is comparatively new—it was passed by Congress in 1913—but since the time of Jamestown's settlement and the arrival of the Pilgrims in Massachusetts, Americans have contributed taxes in one form or another to pay for important defense and community services.

It was "taxation without representation" that was one of the chief causes of the Revolutionary War. When the war was launched, the colonists had to contribute special taxes to help pay for it.

The Constitution gave Congress the power to levy taxes, and it required that they should be paid in a uniform manner, that is, states should pay according to their population.

In those days, when both the Government and its expenses were minute in comparison with later years, the tax laws were simple and uncomplicated, and the job of collecting taxes, while somewhat expensive, was relatively easy. Duties taken in on liquor alone paid almost all the Government's bills.

That pleasant situation did not last long, however, for when the War of 1812 began, Government expenses soared. Customs duties were raised, but they were not enough. New taxes, called temporary war measures, were levied. They were charged against each state, and based on the census of 1810. Still they brought in only $10,000,000, and 90 per cent of the war's costs had to be met by borrowing from the people.

In 1817, the Government was $127,000,000 in debt, but peace brought great industrial expansion and good business conditions. Income from customs increased until once again it was enough to pay the costs of Government and the Treasury could balance its books. This favorable condition generally endured until the clouds forewarning of the Civil War began to gather.

Even in 1861, after the war had begun, the seriousness of the conflict was not fully appreciated. It was thought that the war could be financed by the traditional, time-tested methods of borrowing.

How mistaken Congress had been in this belief was soon seen. As the war progressed Government expenditures increased by leaps and bounds. Drastic new taxes were necessary. First from Congress, on the recommendation of Secretary of the Treasury Salmon P. Chase, came a bill taxing the states, both slave and free, $20,000,000. However, no one had any hope of collecting taxes in southern states under the circumstances. Next came a tax of 3 per cent on all incomes over $800. It was far from enough. The Government found itself plunging into debt at the rate of $2,000,000 a day.

New and broader tax legislation was passed. It taxed all incomes over $600, public utilities, occupations, liquors, tobacco, banks, insurance companies, advertisements, medicines, perfumes, cosmetics, playing cards, and hog slaughtering.

"The principle of this law," declared a Government official, "is like that recommended to the Irishman who visited the Donnybrook Fair: 'Whenever you see a head, hit it.' Whenever we find an article, a product, a trade, a profession, or a source of income, TAX IT!"

In spite of all the heavy taxes inflicted on Americans in the Civil War years, in spite of all the borrowing by the Government, the expenses of the conflict could not be met. In 1864, a new Secretary of the Treasury, William P. Fessenden, sadly surveyed the state of Federal financial affairs. The national debt amounted to more than $3,000,000,000.

As military costs decreased with the arrival of peace, the people clamored for a reduction in the high wartime taxes. This was gradually accomplished during the next ten years. In 1866 the per capita tax—that is, the average tax on every American—had amounted to $8.49. This high point was not to be approached again until 1918, during World War I.

Once more expansion, industrial and agricultural development, and taxes on liquor and tobacco eased the tax burden on the people. Until 1913, nearly 90 per cent of all internal revenue came from levies on distilled spirits, tobacco, and fermented liquor.

In 1909, the need of the Government for more money grew increasingly acute. At last, Congress decided to levy a tax of 1 per cent on the incomes of corporations. This tax was labeled an excise tax on the privilege of doing business.

As the corporation tax law began to take effect, the demand for a tax on personal incomes of individuals increased. Businessmen were especially insistent that it be enacted. The result was the Sixteenth Amendment to the Constitution, and under it taxes were imposed both on individuals and on corporations.

World War I sent Government expenses to unprecedented heights. Taxes were increased and new laws were passed. Telephone calls, telegrams, and excess profits were taxed. Still it was estimated that internal revenue was no more than enough to pay one third of the war's cost. Two thirds had to be defrayed with loans.

Never after this was the United States in a position where it could hope to pay off its national debt. Some wartime taxes were repealed after the Armistice of 1918, and during the 1920's the Government enjoyed a period of taking in more money than it paid out. The surplus went toward cutting the public debt, but it was far from being enough to wipe it out.

Prohibition brought the Internal Revenue Service an enduring headache. Americans simply refused to obey the law, and respectable people who never in their lives had committed a crime made liquor, beer, and bathtub gin. Enforcement was an impossibility, but the Service spared neither efforts nor money in attempting it. In the year 1925 alone, several thousand agents went after the scofflaws. More than 77,000 arrests were made and $11,200,000 worth of property was confiscated. In addition, 7 agents were killed while apprehending bootleggers.

The headache of the prohibition era could not be compared,

however, with that which came with the Great Depression of 1929, for with it came terrible heartache and suffering.

The surpluses in income which the Government had enjoyed during a few prosperous years now ceased. They were supplanted with immense and tragic new demands by a suffering nation. In 1932 Government income was the lowest it had been in fifteen years, yet the need for money was greater than it had ever been in a time of peace.

The repeal of prohibition helped some, bringing in an annual half a billion dollars in revenues on liquors and spirits. The Agricultural Adjustment Act and subsidiary legislation brought in another half billion.

But a whole new theory of social legislation had come into being, bringing the so-called "pump-priming" program. Its doctrine called for increasing government expenditures to improve the purchasing power of the people. A flood of New Deal legislation to give reality to the theory was passed by the Congress.

Public works programs, unemployment insurance, and old age and disability insurance financed through funds collected in taxes on both employers and employees were established by law.

The wounds of the Depression had not completely healed before World War II cast its pall over the earth. Once again taxes had to be drastically increased, and, as had been the case in all other wars, they were insufficient to pay more than a small part of the conflict's costs. Each day the Government was spending more money than it would have needed to operate an entire year a decade or two before. Loans raised the national debt until it had reached proportions that were incomprehensible to most people.

Even the boom times of the postwar years brought insufficient income to balance the Federal budget. In a time of so-called peace, the nation went further into debt. The per capita tax rate when the war ended was $312.13. In 1960, after years of intervening peace, it was $508.37.

The work of the Internal Revenue Service is greater and more complicated now than at any time in history. Inasmuch as every penny of revenue is desperately needed by the Government, efficiency in the collection of taxes is of paramount importance.

The burdens of its investigators and collectors are not lightened by the antics of people who go berserk at the thought of paying taxes. Switchboard operators of the Service are frequently cursed and insulted by anonymous telephone callers. Obscene letters, rarely signed, pour into the Washington headquarters and are turned over to postal inspectors.

But all the abuse and the attacks poured on them have failed to shake an important conviction held by the Service agents. It is that Americans, collectively and individually, comprise the most honest citizenry on earth. Years of examining income tax returns has taught them the truth of this belief.

Unfortunately there are persons and groups who are convinced they can cheat on their income taxes and get away with it. Very few succeed to any great extent.

Income tax agents know every trick in the cheaters' book, and they know where to look for violations. Their confidence in the integrity of Americans does not blind them, nor does it preclude them from being constantly on guard. Agents watch newspapers for the names of sweepstakes winners, or reports of robberies of cash in homes. They make sure the person who won on the horses pays Uncle Sam his just share. And they take the trouble to find out whether the homeowner whose cash was stolen had reported it on his income tax. They watch the flood of forms which descend on the Service's offices, because some misguided and unscrupulous persons have indulged in what is called the "mass-refund racket." These dishonest persons file batches of fake income tax returns, claim they have overpaid their taxes, and demand refunds.

One man wanted to know how he could deduct from his income tax the blood he had given to a blood bank. Another tried to pay his tax with a credit card. The agents always chuckle happily when a young lady appears and says she needs a new form, and they delight in telling you that one of the Service's offices is located at Capitol and Gaines streets.

On the shoulders of the agents attached to the Intelligence Division of the Internal Revenue Service falls the dangerous and difficult work of catching tax cheaters. They are experts at locating hidden evidence and are skilled in determining the true income of an individual or a company attempting to conceal it.

In numerous cases the intelligence agents have succeeded in putting behind bars gangsters who had defeated the efforts of the police. One of the most notorious of these was Al Capone. The agents confiscated Capone's armored car and turned it over to the Secret Service, which used it to protect President Roosevelt. When he was told that he was riding in the gangster's automobile, Mr. Roosevelt said: "I hope Mr. Capone doesn't mind."

Reports of intelligence agents often read like outlines of detective stories. They tell:

—Of a whisky distiller and two attorneys who created 37 foreign corporations to make it appear that $20,000,000 in profits from whisky had been made outside the United States and therefore could not be taxed.

—Of waiters, bellhops, and porters who failed to report all the cash they took in from customers.

—Of gambling room operators who not only cheated with dice and cards but with a pencil in making out their income tax returns.

—Of an unemployed coal miner who filed 17 duplicate income tax returns in the hope of getting refund checks on them.

—Of an attorney, thought to be respectable, who received income from pinball machines and numbers games but did not bother to report it.

—Of a stock exchange clerk who traded in securities under several names but forgot to tell the Service about his profits.

—Of the owner of 11 motion picture theaters who did not report all the money he took in from selling tickets.

—Of a former judge who attempted to hide his interest in 2 saloons.

—Of a registered nurse who received $730,000 in "gifts" from her employer but forgot to mention them to the Internal Revenue Service.

There is a great difference, of course, between petty "chiselers" and large-scale cheaters, and the intelligence agents take this into consideration. They do not want to put in jail the man who forgot to list the $10 he won in a friendly card game with neighbors, but if they find out about it, they insist that he pay a tax on it. In the eyes of the agents income is income, and income is taxable. In the case of the $10 the agents may be willing to believe that the man simply forgot it, and if he pays, nothing more is said. They don't have this kindly feeling for a gangster or businessman who keeps dishonest books.

There are, in reality, relatively few individual Americans or companies which fall into the criminal category, those who deliberately and with premeditation scheme to defraud the Treasury by evading payment of their income tax. In a recent year only 1,553 taxpayers in all the United States were convicted and sentenced for this crime—a small percentage, indeed, out of 94,000,000 Federal taxpayers.

The Service admits that many others probably escaped detection simply because of the impossibility of examining and checking every tax return. Only about 1 in every 20 can be

The cornerstone is of historic interest. Ironically, it was laid by President Andrew Jackson, who had no liking for either banks or bankers. President Jackson put into it a small satin-lined case containing a lock of golden hair that had been snipped from the head of the infant daughter of his confidential adviser and secretary, who was Mrs. Jackson's nephew. The girl, Mary Emily Donelson, grew up to work for the Treasury.

As the building was enlarged, it moved around and over the cornerstone, entombing it. Now all that can be said is that it must be "down there someplace," forever inaccessible under the great granite pile.

When the famous designer and military engineer Pierre Charles L'Enfant drew the plans for the new national city of Washington, he set aside a site for a treasury building. It was to stand to the east of the President's house, facing the Mall, which cut a wide swath through the heart of the city.

The first Treasury Building was ready for occupancy in 1800, when the capital of the United States was moved from Philadelphia to Washington. The sixty-nine employees of the Treasury Department who moved into it were obliged to share the building with the seven employees who comprised the Department of State, and with several others from the Navy Department.

In the very next year fire badly damaged the building. Repairs were made, but it seemed that Fate had decreed for it a short life. In 1814, during the War of 1812, invading British troops surged up Pennsylvania Avenue, leaving the House of Congress in flames behind them. Next they set fire both to the Treasury and to the White House.

Fire appeared to be a greater enemy of the Treasury Department than counterfeiters or smugglers. In 1833 the Treasury Building which had been built after the War of 1812 was leveled by flames. Furious, President Jackson, who had watched the fire from a White House window, launched an exhaustive investigation. It resulted in the arrest of two brothers who were charged with arson.

The brothers had become involved in a scheme to defraud the Treasury Department. Fearful of being discovered, they had decided to destroy certain papers which might convict them. Early in the morning of March 31, 1833, they broke into the Treasury Building and set fire to the incriminating records. The fire spread until it was out of hand, and before it could be stopped, the entire structure and all its contents had been destroyed. One of the brothers was sentenced to ten years in prison, but the other was acquitted after four trials.

For the next three years the Treasury had no home of its own, but on July 4, 1836, Congress authorized the construction of a "fireproof building of such dimensions as may be required for the present and future accommodations" of the Treasury Department.

The building that was completed in 1842 was an imposing structure for the time, but it fell far short of providing accommodations for the future, as Congress had ordered. Now its 150 rooms are a small part of the Treasury Building's east wing. The south wing of the present building was completed in 1861. More room was soon needed. The Department of State was ousted from its building north of the Treasury, and the immense north wing of the present Treasury Building was completed by 1869.

After more than a third of a century, during which it was periodically expanded and its cornerstone lost, the Treasury Building at last became the magnificent structure that the department originally had intended to construct.

L'Enfant's design, however, had been violated. He had planned to leave unobstructed the view from the White House to the Capitol, along Pennsylvania Avenue. In its growth the Treasury Building had cut off that view.

L'Enfant also had proposed to have all Government buildings facing the Mall, and in accordance with this plan the front entrances of the Treasury and the White House were placed on their south sides. These are the historical front entrances of both structures, but as the city grew about them, convenience and accessibility made the north doors the main entrances, and so they are considered today.

Most of the stone used in the Treasury Building was quarried on Dix Island, near Rockland, Maine, and brought to Washington in sailing vessels. The façades are adorned by monolithic columns of the Ionic order. Each column is 36 feet high, and weighs about 30 tons. Of these columns 34 stand on the Fifteenth Street side of the building and 30 form a colonnade 341 feet in length. There are 18 columns on the west side, and 10 each on the north and south sides.

The statue of Alexander Hamilton, first Secretary of the Treasury, stands in the south patio of the building. In the north patio is a large bronze statue of Albert Gallatin, who served as Secretary of the Treasury longer than any other man. At the north and south ends are rose gardens, and lawns and magnolia trees grace the west side.

As you enter the Treasury Building you are quickly reminded that it is very old. The deeply worn stone steps leading to all floors account the many years they were used before elevators were installed. The elevators themselves may be classed as collector's items. Some have been in use since the turn of the century. Only one can be described as truly modern, and it was installed in 1959. Plans have been drawn for replacing all of them with automatic self-operating cars.

Although electricity and steam heat have long been used, evidence of the early lighting and heating systems still remains. You can see where old oil lamps were hung. There are many fireplaces, and some of them are still usable. Oil paintings—portraits, seascapes, and landscapes—are hung throughout the building, and with the old-fashioned furniture and paneled walls, they give some of the rooms the air of a colonial New England banking house. It is difficult to clean the high ceilings and they sometimes wear coats of dust, an occasional corner decorated with a cobweb. The floors of the executive suites are covered with soft, old rugs. The halls leading to them are lined with pilasters painted a rich, soft green, the green of the bills which are stacked in the vaults in neat packages. Washington has long, humid summers, and air conditioning came to the relief of Treasury employees only a few years ago. Before that time, slatted doors permitted some air to circulate through sweltering rooms. The slatted doors are still there, and on walking along some corridors you might think you were passing staterooms on an old-fashioned steamer in the Orient.

As if they felt more secure next to so much money, starlings until recently roosted by the thousands at night on the Treasury Building ledges and cornices. Walking along the street beneath them was extremely hazardous. All manner of tricks were used in an effort to induce the noisy little birds to select another gathering place, but they stubbornly refused to be dislodged. At last electric wires were strung along the roosts, but many of the starlings have learned how to avoid getting a shock, although some have become discouraged and have departed for safer roosts.

In the basement of the Treasury Building are 15 vaults ranging in size from 10 by 16 feet to 50 by 90 feet. At one time all the Government's wealth—including its stocks of opium—was stored in them, but that is not true today. Millions are locked up in them every night, but they hold no silver or gold bullion as they once did. Now the Treasury keeps the larger part of its money in Federal Reserve and private banks throughout the country. In the basement, also, is a pistol range used by the Secret Service and other Treasury agents to practice their marksmanship. During World War II one of the vaults was fitted out as an air raid shelter for the use of

President Roosevelt. An underground passage led directly into it from the White House.

The vaults and the building are protected by the Treasury Guard Force, also a branch of the Secret Service. It consists of 70 uniformed men especially trained to fight the Treasury's historic nemesis—fire. Breaking into the building, as it was accomplished in President Jackson's day, would be quite impossible. The guards are aided by an electronic protection system. The slightest attempt to tamper with locks, doors, and windows, or even the granite walls, would bring Secret Service agents, Treasury guards, and the Washington police quickly to the scene.

Many events not connected with money have taken place in the Treasury Building. President Andrew Johnson established his office in it immediately after the assassination of President Lincoln so that Mrs. Lincoln would not be hurried in moving out of the White House.

The immense Cash Room was the scene of President Ulysses S. Grant's first inaugural ball, on March 4, 1869.

The First Baptist Church of Washington held its first meeting in the building, and in recent years it has held commemorative meetings on the great south steps. The steps were the scene of massive bond rallies led by world-famous persons during both world wars, and they also have been used for launching Community Chest and other fund drives.

Magnificent is the word that best describes the great Cash Room, which is in the north end of the building. Walls, window frames, and doors are constructed of solid marble. Two stories in height, the Cash Room maintains an atmosphere of dignity and antiquity, although the millions of dollars handled there each day display a charm that is as modern as the present moment.

People who work in the Treasury Building cherish its traditions and often vigorously oppose any change. If some structural improvement should be proposed, everyone takes an interest in the matter, and more often than not, strong opposition arises. Some Treasury people even resisted the plan to clean and bird-proof the building, even though the thousands of pigeons and starlings attached to it were a frightful nuisance.

For more than a hundred years after it was built the Treasury Building had no name on it. When, in 1957, it was proposed that a name should be displayed, vigorous arguments ensued. Some Treasury people thought a name unnecessary. Another argument revolved around the question of the Treasury's proper name, as it had been called both the Department of the Treasury and the Treasury Department since 1789. But Secretary of the Treasury George M. Humphrey, by nature a thrifty man, decided that the shorter name—Treasury Department—was preferable.

The office of the Secretary of the Treasury is on the third floor. It is a large, dignified, richly furnished suite with a fine view of the White House. Two signs near the entrance ask: "Quiet Please." In the waiting room the countenances of two former Secretaries, George M. Humphrey and Henry Morgenthau, Jr.—whose ideas on the subject of finance were poles apart—gaze amicably enough at each other from their frames. The Secretary's suite is graced with a lovely black marble fireplace. Portraits of other secretaries—Alexander Hamilton, Robert B. Anderson, John Snyder, and Albert Gallatin—adorn the walls in a display that suggests a conglomeration of policies involving money. The entire group of rooms might be likened to a stage set for a drama about a fine old New England mansion.

The present occupant of the Secretary's office, Douglas Dillon, is a tall aristocrat who looks completely comfortable and at home behind his big desk. Although a Democratic administration rules the Government, he is a Republican.

President Kennedy appointed him because of his outstanding ability as a banker and his long experience in problems related to national and international finance.

Before becoming Secretary of the Treasury on January 21, 1961, Douglas Dillon was Under Secretary of State for Economic Affairs. He receives a salary of $25,000 a year. As an investment banker, which is his business in private life, he would have an income many times larger. Like numerous other leaders in the Government, Secretary Dillon is contributing his services and his extraordinary ability to his country at a great personal sacrifice.

One might think that being the head of a Government department that employs 82,000 civilian men and women, and being responsible for the activities of hundreds of secret agents and a navy—the Coast Guard—larger than that of many foreign nations, would be enough for any man. But the Government thinks not. Like all members of the President's Cabinet, the Secretary of the Treasury carries an enormous burden of responsibilities in addition to those of his own office.

Secretary Dillon is chief financial adviser to the President, and United States governor of various international organizations, the International Bank for Reconstruction and Development, the International Monetary Fund, and the Inter-American Development Bank. He is a member of the boards of trustees of the Postal Savings System, the Smithsonian Institution, and the National Gallery of Art, honorary treasurer of the National Red Cross, and a trustee or board member of numerous other important Federal Government organizations.

"The boss," said a Treasury executive, "has more official hats than he can possibly wear."

Secretary Dillon is a member of a wealthy family, but not long ago he admitted that he had never closely examined a piece of United States currency until his own name began to appear on it as Secretary of the Treasury. This habit of carelessness, which he had in common with millions of Americans, did not suggest that he was not interested in it. It meant, just as it does to most people, that he had unqualified faith in American money. Faith in the American dollar, he believes, is the cement that binds together the great alliance of the Free World, and he has pledged himself to do all in his power to see that that faith is never damaged.

SECRETARIES OF THE TREASURY

Presidents	Secretaries	Term of Service	
		From	To
WASHINGTON	Alexander Hamilton, New York	Sept. 11, 1789	Jan. 31, 1795
	Oliver Wolcott, Connecticut	Feb. 3, 1795	March 3, 1797
ADAMS, JOHN	Oliver Wolcott, Connecticut	March 4, 1797	Dec. 31, 1800
	Samuel Dexter, Massachusetts	Jan. 1, 1801	March 3, 1801
JEFFERSON	Samuel Dexter, Massachusetts	March 4, 1801	May 13, 1801
	Albert Gallatin, Pennsylvania	May 14, 1801	March 3, 1809
MADISON	Albert Gallatin, Pennsylvania	March 4, 1809	Feb. 8, 1814
	George W. Campbell, Tennessee	Feb. 9, 1814	Oct. 5, 1814
	Alexander J. Dallas, Pennsylvania	Oct. 6, 1814	Oct. 21, 1816
	William H. Crawford, Georgia	Oct. 22, 1816	March 3, 1817
MONROE	William H. Crawford, Georgia	March 4, 1817	March 6, 1825
ADAMS, J. Q.	Richard Rush, Pennsylvania	March 7, 1825	March 5, 1829
JACKSON	Samuel D. Ingham, Pennsylvania	March 6, 1829	June 20, 1831
	Louis McLane, Delaware	Aug. 8, 1831	May 28, 1833
	Wm. J. Duane, Pennsylvania	May 29, 1833	Sept. 22, 1833
	Roger B. Taney, Maryland	Sept. 23, 1833	June 25, 1834
	Levi Woodbury, New Hampshire	July 1, 1834	March 3, 1837
VAN BUREN	Levi Woodbury, New Hampshire	March 4, 1837	March 3, 1841

HARRISON	Thomas Ewing, Ohio	March 6, 1841	April 4, 1841
TYLER	Thomas Ewing, Ohio	April 5, 1841	Sept. 11, 1841
	Walter Forward, Pennsylvania	Sept. 13, 1841	March 1, 1843
	John C. Spencer, New York	March 8, 1843	May 2, 1844
	George M. Bibb, Kentucky	July 4, 1844	March 4, 1845
POLK	George M. Bibb, Kentucky	March 5, 1845	March 7, 1845
	Robert J. Walker, Mississippi	March 8, 1845	March 5, 1849
TAYLOR	William M. Meredith, Pennsylvania	March 8, 1849	July 9, 1850
FILLMORE	William M. Meredith, Pennsylvania	July 10, 1850	July 22, 1850
	Thomas Corwin, Ohio	July 23, 1850	March 6, 1853
PIERCE	James Guthrie, Kentucky	March 7, 1853	March 6, 1857
BUCHANAN	Howell Cobb, Georgia	March 7, 1857	Dec. 8, 1860
	Philip F. Thomas, Maryland	Dec. 12, 1860	Jan. 14, 1861
	John A. Dix, New York	Jan. 15, 1861	March 6, 1861
LINCOLN	Salmon P. Chase, Ohio	March 7, 1861	June 30, 1864
	William P. Fessenden, Maine	July 5, 1864	March 3, 1865
	Hugh McCulloch, Indiana	March 9, 1865	April 15, 1865
JOHNSON	Hugh McCulloch, Indiana	April 16, 1865	March 3, 1869
GRANT	Geo. S. Boutwell, Massachusetts	March 12, 1869	March 16, 1873
	William A. Richardson, Massachusetts	March 17, 1873	June 3, 1874
	Benjamin H. Bristow, Kentucky	June 4, 1874	June 20, 1876
	Lot M. Morrill, Maine	July 7, 1876	March 3, 1877

SECRETARIES OF THE TREASURY (*Continued*)

Presidents	Secretaries	Term of Service	
		From	To
HAYES	Lot M. Morrill, Maine	March 4, 1877	March 9, 1877
	John Sherman, Ohio	March 10, 1877	March 3, 1881
GARFIELD	William Windom, Minnesota	March 8, 1881	Sept. 19, 1881
ARTHUR	William Windom, Minnesota	Sept. 20, 1881	Nov. 13, 1881
	Charles J. Folger, New York	Nov. 14, 1881	Sept. 4, 1884
	Walter Q. Gresham, Indiana	Sept. 25, 1884	Oct. 30, 1884
	Hugh McCulloch, Indiana	Oct. 31, 1884	March 3, 1885
CLEVELAND	Hugh McCulloch, Indiana	March 4, 1885	March 7, 1885
	Daniel Manning, New York	March 8, 1885	March 31, 1887
	Charles S. Fairchild, New York	April 1, 1887	March 3, 1889
HARRISON	Charles S. Fairchild, New York	March 4, 1889	March 6, 1889
	William Windom, Minnesota	March 7, 1889	Jan. 29, 1891
	Charles Foster, Ohio	Feb. 25, 1891	March 3, 1893
CLEVELAND	Charles Foster, Ohio	March 4, 1893	March 6, 1893
	John G. Carlisle, Kentucky	March 7, 1893	March 3, 1897
McKINLEY	John G. Carlisle, Kentucky	March 4, 1897	March 5, 1897
	Lyman J. Gage, Illinois	March 6, 1897	Sept. 14, 1901
ROOSEVELT, T.	Lyman J. Gage, Illinois	Sept. 15, 1901	Jan. 31, 1902
	L. M. Shaw, Iowa	Feb. 1, 1902	March 3, 1907
	G. B. Cortelyou, New York	March 4, 1907	March 7, 1909

TAFT	Franklin MacVeagh, Illinois	March 8, 1909	March 5, 1913
WILSON	W. G. McAdoo, New York	March 6, 1913	Dec. 15, 1918
	Carter Glass, Virginia	Dec. 16, 1918	Feb. 1, 1920
	David F. Houston, Missouri	Feb. 2, 1920	March 3, 1921
HARDING	Andrew W. Mellon, Pennsylvania	March 4, 1921	Aug. 2, 1923
COOLIDGE	Andrew W. Mellon, Pennsylvania	Aug. 3, 1923	March 3, 1929
HOOVER	Andrew W. Mellon, Pennsylvania	March 4, 1929	Feb. 12, 1932
	Ogden L. Mills, New York	Feb. 13, 1932	March 4, 1933
ROOSEVELT, F. D.	William H. Woodin, New York	March 5, 1933	Dec. 31, 1933
	Henry Morgenthau, Jr., New York	Jan. 1, 1934	April 12, 1945
TRUMAN	Henry Morgenthau, Jr., New York	April 13, 1945	July 22, 1945
	Fred M. Vinson, Kentucky	July 23, 1945	June 23, 1946
	John W. Snyder, Missouri	June 25, 1946	Jan. 20, 1953
EISENHOWER	George M. Humphrey, Ohio	Jan. 21, 1953	July 29, 1957
	Robert B. Anderson, Connecticut	July 29, 1957	Jan. 20, 1961
KENNEDY	Douglas Dillon, New Jersey	Jan. 21, 1961